The Power Of People Skills 2 In 1

How To Have Great Conversations Without Pretending To Be Someone Else

By

John Guzman

Table of Contents

People Skills Secrets

The Art Of People Skills

Chapter 4: Improving Your Conversations 197

Chapter 5: Listening Skills..............230

People Skills Secrets

How To Become Comfortable To Talk To Anyone And Make Friends Without Being Awkward

By

John Guzman

Introduction

You try to talk to someone and your voice gets stuck in your throat. You walk away, humiliated and frustrated at your lack of social skills. If you learned some real people skills, you would have conversations more easily, find friends left and right, and even stumble upon greater opportunities in life.

I should know all about this. As a shy introvert unable to talk to people, I was missing out on life quite a lot. I realized that I needed to improve my people skills if I wanted to work in customer service, which was my first job. Through months of practice and studying research about social skills, I finally found the formula that enabled me to become comfortable with people. Now I'm not shy at all and I have many great friends, a huge business network, and luck with getting dates.

If you want to be like me, then you are reading the right book. You can change. The benefits of having social skills are countless. Think landing jobs at the first interview, making friends with one conversation, and avoiding awkwardness at parties. Think asking your crush out and getting favors. Think confidence and happiness in your own skin. Your whole future will open right at your feet.

The truth is, you can't survive without social skills because humans are a social species. You must learn how to interact. This book will show you how to do just that. From starting conversations to getting over your fears, this book will help you develop the skills that will get you far in life.

I promise that by the end of this book, you will be a new person. Your relationships and self-confidence will both improve. But you must do your part – you must read this book and actually use the information contained!

If you don't do this now, you can expect a lifetime of

regrets, shyness, and feeling passed over for every promotion. Leadership opportunities, great friendships, and successful business will all be unavailable. You must start building these vital skills immediately.

So, what are you waiting for? Start on your journey to become a social people person!

Chapter 1: The Right Mindset To Make Friends

Like everything in life, mind is over matter. Your mindset drives how you act and how you present yourself to others [1]. Therefore, you must have a certain mindset to make friends.

All Kinds Of Worries

What is wrong with your mindset now? The answer requires some introspection. Most people can't make friends due to some kind of worry that chokes them up. They give off a sense of nervousness and fear, which others find off-putting. They may even be so nervous that they don't even try to talk to people at all. The result is social awkwardness driven by fear. Obviously, the solution is getting rid of the fear, but first you must identify what that fear is.

I Am Too Old

Or I am too fat, I am too ugly, I am too stupid. There are a million different ways to express the same fear: that you are not good enough for other people. You find something you don't like about yourself and magnify it into an issue that seems completely insurmountable. You assume others won't like you because of whatever this insecurity is.

Chances are, other people don't like you, but it has nothing to do with your insecurity; it has to do with the fact that you make it very clear you are not confident in your own skin. People can sense that, and they run away because they desire confidence [1].

Your insecurities and flaws are usually more pronounced to you than to others [2]. You notice what is wrong with you and make it a whole part of your identity. Other people might notice your flaws, but they are not going to refuse to be friends with you because of them. They want to see confidence.

In a study, participants were asked to rate their fatness. Most people rated themselves as at least two-thirds wider than they really were [2]. This was most pronounced in women, but it was true of men as well. The point of this study was to prove that our flaws are smaller in the eyes of others. We tend to magnify our flaws, including our weight, and we look better to others than we do to ourselves.

The key to getting over this is learning to accept and love yourself. It also involves realizing that other people don't judge you as harshly as you judge yourself. Others tend to be too wrapped up in their own problems to magnify your flaws. The exception may be someone working in a modeling agency or

Anxiety Because Of Failure

Maybe in the past you tried to make friends and they rebuffed you. Now you are scared to try again. The truth is that some people are unkind or going through bad things in life, so they don't respond well to your attempts to make friends. You can't let that prevent you from trying again.

Many people use something called generalizing, or globalizing [3]. This is where they base their judgments of others on one person or one experience. You are globalizing everyone you could make friends with based on the one person or group of people who did not respond well to your friendliness. That prevents you from meeting the people out there who might embrace you as a friend.

Consider if you were bullied in school and now you are not very social. The thing is, people tend to grow up after school and leave behind that juvenile hostility. In the real world, you can meet adults who will not reject you as your high school peers did. So, don't overgeneralize and assume everyone is like your high school bullies.

Shyness

Some people suffer from shyness. Some even go on to develop social anxiety. While these two things are not the same, they are similar in that they induce irrational fear of speaking to others and having social interactions. These issues may be caused by a past trauma, an abusive childhood, or simply a chemical imbalance in the brain.

If you find yourself taking a different route home just to avoid talking to your neighbor, dropping eye contact, and shunning social engagement, you may suffer from social anxiety. This is a mental disorder that can be treated with cognitive behavioral therapy, social anxiety coping groups, and social skills practice sessions. It may even be treated by medication. It's time to seek help to improve your life with social skills and normal social interactions.

The Confident Mindset

Confidence is attractive, to the point where people seek it in others [1]. If you are confident, then you let others know that nothing is wrong. Then they can feel at ease. The entire group is content, and socializing can take place unimpeded. This stems from our evolutionary roots, when we needed to feel at peace from threats like lions and wolves. While our world may be safer in some ways now, that instinct lingers on, permeating our social atmosphere.

In fact, confidence is so attractive that people will make decisions based on the confidence that they detect in another [1]. Basically, being confident makes you someone that others look up to and turn to for guidance. You make people feel safe as if you are their leader when you project confidence. Not projecting confidence leads to discouraging people from making decisions [1].

From this, you can gather that having a confident

mindset is the right mindset for making friends.

Be Less Self-Absorbed

To make friends, your mindset must embrace social interaction and be interested in others. Only then do you show others that you like them and want to hang out. This makes them like you, and thus friendships are cemented.

Imagine the most self-centered person in your office or social life. She or he talks on and on, and never asks other people what they are feeling or thinking. She/he never remembers names and doesn't talk about other people or ask how their days are going. No one really likes him/her; they tolerate him/her with eye rolls. Well, this is a prime example of a person with few friends because of her high level of self-absorption.

It's time to put yourself aside and quit talking about

yourself incessantly. You certainly can mention things about yourself, but you need to turn your focus outward. This is especially difficult for introverts but it's crucial. Talk to people and ask them about themselves. That will create far more friendships than talking about yourself.

This means that you need to remember names and birthdays. You need to ask someone, "How was your day?" Ask about a person's hobbies. And really listen when they answer you. Stop thinking about yourself and think of others, and you will get great results.

"That lady who never shuts up in the adjacent cubicle never talks about anybody else and she has friends," you might say. The thing is, she doesn't really. She injects herself into conversations, so it seems like she has people to talk to. But really, everyone ignores her. She has no true friends.

Be Willing To Venture Out Of Your Comfort Zone

Your comfort zone is a safe place where you hide. In it, you don't try new things or meet new people. That's great except that it ensures your life never changes in any way. Only when you venture out of this safe space and start experimenting with what life has to offer you will you begin to make friends.

In your little bubble, you don't cross paths with many new people. You also don't have much to relate on with new people. But when you try something new, you put yourself out there, crossing paths and developing things to talk about. Plus, you seem more interesting and more confident because you are willing to explore the world.

Many people claim that making friends as an adult is hard. It's only hard because adults tend to settle into a rut. They keep the friends they have and don't bother to make new ones; they have their hobbies and their routines and don't vary much. Thus, they don't meet and interact with new people, and they don't make new friends. However, you can change that by being willing to put yourself out there.

Always Be Willing To Talk First

People often won't come to you and talk first. The reason is explained before: they are set in their ways. Why talk to someone new? Some of them may be just as shy as you. Only when you speak first do you make people notice you and respond.

Therefore, you must change your mindset to one that enables you to speak first. You must be willing and ready to start new conversations with new people. Chat with the cashier at the convenience store, the barista at your favorite coffeehouse, the bartender making your drink. Say hi to your co-worker and ask him how his weekend trip went. Call your old friends first to catch up.

Being the first to speak puts you in the unique position to control and steer the interaction. You can make someone notice you, respond to you, and realize who you are. You just opened a pathway to a potential friendship.

Always Look For Things In Common

People like that which is similar to them [4]. They seek things in common because it makes them feel comfortable and safe by inducing similar neural activity [4]. When a person finds something in common with you, he or she automatically likes you more and has more to talk about with you. The bond strengthens based purely on that single commonality. Similarities may range from having the same favorite basketball team or sharing a mutual friend.

So, when you are meeting a new person, you must have the mindset to create bonds over similarities, not divisions over differences. Instead of looking for ways to disagree about politics or differ in hobbies, look for ways to share a bond. Find something you two share, even if it isn't much.

Chapter 2: Developing The Right Mindset To Make Friends

Now that you know the right mindset, you may still wonder how to go about building it. After all, just reading about a mindset doesn't cause you to acquire it. It takes some work to bring your mindset up to standards as one that relates to others and makes friends easily.

How To Build Confidence

Your insecurities are a part of you. You can't just ignore them. Instead, try to negate them.

"I'm fat," your mind says. Tell your mind, "OK, I weigh a little bit. But I still have a pretty face and I love my curves! I'm also a really great person."

"I'm old," you think. Tell yourself, "I have a lot more wisdom under my belt and I have had a lot of life experience. I'm full of cool stories."

Find things that make you feel not good enough. Then negate them with positives. There is always something good about you to outweigh the negative. This is not to say that you have nothing negative about you – we all do. But these negatives can't be at the forefront of your mind, stopping you from making friends, because you are guaranteed to have good traits too.

Also, try to see how little these negative things really matter. Is a true friend going to care overly much that you have a weight problem or are a bit older than he or she is? Are other people as obsessed about your flaws as you are, or are they more likely to ignore them because they are focused on their own flaws? The correct answer is the latter. People don't notice or care about your flaws as much as you do [2].

Make a list of the good things you do each day. Make

another list of the good things about yourself. These two lists can help you see that you are not all bad. There are plenty of things to love about yourself.

Start to work on your self-talk. This is how you talk to yourself. What does your inner monologue sound like? If it has a lot of "You always do this," "You will just fail again," "You are so [insert negative adjective]," or "You are not good enough, I hate you!", then it's time for a change. Focus on chasing those self-hating thoughts with more positive ones. "I can do it!" "I'm a good person." "I think I will do well at this."

Approach things from a more solution-oriented mindset as well. Should you fail at something, think, "What can I learn from this to make the results better next time?" If you think you can't do something, think how you can learn how to do it right. If you have a flaw you hate, think how you can improve it and take those steps.

Another tip is to set up a series of little goals that you can achieve. As you achieve them, your belief in yourself grows. The next thing you know, you are tackling much bigger and more significant goals. Start just with what you can do today to prevent yourself from feeling overwhelmed. Then, move on to grander goals.

Finally, stop comparing yourself to some standard set by someone else or yourself. Your body is not made to look like a Victoria Secret Angel's; that's OK. You are not supposed to have everything figured out by any age; you can screw up now and then. People tend to impose comparisons on you, or you tend to impose them on yourself. You look to others for models of how to be and then feel awful when you fall short. It's time to stop those thoughts as you start thinking them. Remind yourself that you are a unique person with a unique set of life circumstances, so of course you will be different. Comparisons are not accurate and not helpful.

As you do these things, you start to love yourself. That makes you more confident. Confidence comes from within, as you start to see the good in yourself and embrace it without letting the bad in yourself ruin your entire self-image. You start to believe that you can do things and you are worthy of better than what you have been getting in the past.

How To Tackle Anxiety/Shyness

If the idea of meeting new people makes your knees knock together, you are far from alone. A lot of people have social anxiety or shyness – an estimated 15 million adults in the United States, as a matter of fact [5].

Social anxiety can be addressed with cognitive behavioral therapy, which you can perform on yourself. Get a CBT workbook on Amazon and begin to address the thinking that makes you so socially anxious. This helps you rewire your brain so that you talk and act differently, favoring helpful and positive thoughts over negative, harmful ones.

If social anxiety incapacitates you to the point that you can't leave the house or make eye contact with anyone, then you need some help. Social anxiety can be debilitating but you can mitigate that. Therapy and medications usually work well to restore your quality of life. Even if you feel that you are not incapacitated by social anxiety, getting help is not a bad thing.

Shyness can be overcome simply with practice. You can start by practicing in a mirror. When you feel more confident with what to say, start to practice at places like bars or coffee shops where you don't know anyone. Make small talk with the barista, for instance. With practice, your confidence grows, and you start to navigate social interactions more confidently and securely [6].

You should also make yourself more vulnerable. By admitting to having emotions, you can find points to relate to people on [4]. If a woman is telling you that her dog died, you can empathize and create more of a connection. You can even mention how your dog died once too. This is just an example of how being vulnerable can help you shed your shyness and start to actually relate to people. Shyness tends to make you freeze up and try to act perfect, which in turn makes you seem unnatural. Being vulnerable helps you relax and bond with people better.

Being vulnerable also entails being your authentic self. You can't focus on being perfect or you will blow it because no one is perfect. You also can't focus on your flaws, or you will become self-conscious and shy as a result. Instead, you must think, "I am who I am. Take me or leave me." This powerful attitude comes across as confidence because it is the very essence of confidence. Other people will see it and like you more. If you act self-consciously, then you draw attention to your flaws and put other people off. Avoid being self-conscious or apologizing for yourself; just be you, no apologies.

Another tip is to use powerful, confident body language, AKA power posing [7]. Power posing involves having an open body language. You don't cross your arms or legs, shrink into a chair, or turn away from people. Rather, you face them squarely, with your arms and legs open. You keep your head high and your neck and back straight. You walk with purpose, swinging your arms wide. When on a couch or chair, relax into it and place your arms over the back of it. These little things tell people that you are one confident person and you already know how that helps you gain friends. By using a power pose at all times, you make others respect you more, which leads to positive social interactions. As a result, you forget your shyness as people come to you.

Finally, stop focusing on the things that make you feel

afraid or insecure. Focus instead on other people. Listen to them and think of things to say. This keeps your mind off its anxiety and helps you stay present in the conversation. That will do you wonders.

The more you talk and the more you get into a conversation, the more relaxed and confident you become. That also makes you more vulnerable – more authentic. Shyness will trickle away with practice [6].

How To Stay Relaxed In Every Situation

If social situations make you nervous, you can't be expected to just relax and be at ease. But with some work, you can get there. Being relaxed tells other people that you are OK, so they are OK too; it is that crucial sense of safety that confidence gives others [1].

The first key to relaxation starts with breath. You use

breath calm your body and tell yourself that everything is OK. Your brain responds by reducing the adrenalin that makes you jittery and full of dread. You breathe in through your nose and then out through your mouth. Keep it rhythmic. Start breathing well before a social situation and then breathe through it and you will enjoy much more relaxation. Actors will use breathing before an audition or performance; singers use vocal exercises to achieve this.

Another key is to stop the huge amount of anxious thinking shooting through your brain. You can do this by being mindful of the present situation. Stay aware of what others are saying and what they look like. When your thoughts start to wander toward "How do people here think of me?" and "What am I doing?" draw them back by focusing on someone's face or words. Being mindful is essential to letting go of worries and feeling more at ease.

Mindfulness is basically mental control. You can identify and control your thinking. You will find that a daily mindfulness meditation helps you get this control. The simplest exercise involves staring at a spot on the wall with full concentration. You can't think about anything else. If you do, you gently acknowledge the thought and then bring your attention back to the spot on the wall. With time, this becomes habit that enables you to control your thinking and stay present and relaxed.

Some people use alcohol or drugs to relax. While these things certainly work, the problem is that they make you a fake person in any social situation. People get to know you for the person you are when under the influence of something. Then, if they meet you sober, they are surprised by the change and even put off. Plus, you can make a bad impression if you are always drinking or taking drugs, and you may not be able to use these substances you come to rely on in certain situations that require social skills, such as a job interview. It is far better to let people see the real you. That is the only one to build true connections that go deeper than the effects of drugs and alcohol.

How To Naturally Become More Extroverted

One of the biggest misconceptions about introversion is that introverts are shy. This is not true at all. Introverts are simply people who get energy from within, not from others. Therefore, they are great at working alone or being alone, and may even need alone time to recharge. However, they are not shy by default. Many introverts display extroverted characteristics, being talkative, confident, and outgoing in social situations. Many of them like having friends as well.

The average introvert is a private person. He likes talking about others more than himself. He prefers one-on-one conversations to talking to whole groups of people. Nevertheless, he needs and can perform in social situations. With proper social skills, you can't even tell he's introverted, unless you get to know him well and find out he needs his private time to recharge.

Introverts are not shy, but shy people are introverted. That's the key difference. If you are shy, becoming an extrovert will not help you, nor is it possible. But you can learn social skills that make you a very social introvert. Remain an introvert and be comfortable with who you are, and you will succeed socially. The more comfortable and accepting you are of your introverted characteristics, the better you will do in social situations anyway. Your confidence will bloom from accepting who you really are.

Extroverts are people who draw energy from others. They must work on teams, have friends, and talk to others to be happy. The stereotype is that they are always the life of the party, but in fact, shy extroverts do exist. Shy extroverts crave the attention of others and even need it to thrive, yet they can't build bonds out of fear. They have a unique set of problems that they must overcome by learning proper social skills.

If you are a shy person, it does not matter if you are introverted or extroverted. Shyness is an issue in and of itself. Overcoming shyness has nothing to do with changing your personality type from introvert to extrovert. However, if you want to become more like an extroverted person, it is possible. Observingin and adopting the characteristics of a social extrovert provides the guidelines for being a social and comfortable person.

The Meyer-Briggs personality test uses a series of questions to find your personality type. Out of sixteen types, half are introverted, and half are extroverted. Your personality is fairly static; it will not change with time, nor can you make it change [8]. You are better off accepting your personality type and working with it to be social, as opposed to trying to change it, which is impossible. That is the key to naturally becoming more extroverted in your behavior. If you are an introvert and you embrace that, you can get over social anxiety and shyness, and become a very social and comfortable introvert that other people like. Instead of changing who you are or being fake, you can just learn to talk to people comfortably, relax in social situations, and have a good time without feeling anxious. Get over fear of social situations and get over insecurities to become a social magnet.

Introverts are more than capable of being social and having great social lives. They just need some alone time and they tend to think better alone. Taking some time to recharge and make decisions is important for you to do if you are introverted. On the other hand, extroverts who are shy can grow confident in who they are and learn some social skills, with absolutely no issues barring them from becoming extroverted in behavior.

The main key to becoming more extroverted in your

behavior entails talking more. You just have to talk, that's it. Tell jokes, tell stories, ask people about how they are and what they feel about the current affairs. Making conversation puts you out there and makes people relate to you. You don't hang back in a corner, waiting to be spoken to; you speak to people as if they are already your friends.

Always smile and talk first. That draws people to you. Offer your hand for a firm handshake and introduce yourself first. These small things make people notice you and relate to you. Hanging back in shyness will cause you to be invisible.

You want to speak first often, as well. Say there's an impromptu meeting. Being the first to open your mouth and lead the meeting makes everyone take note of who you are and what you have to say. This is something extroverts do – speaking without permission or fear. They just let out what they are thinking without inhibitions. They enable people to identify with their thoughts and create bonds, and they make themselves heard.

Also, get out more. Introverts like to stay where they are familiar and comfortable, thus causing them to miss out on new social possibilities. Therefore, you must go to new places, such as new bars, new churches, or new book clubs. Try new activities that take you out of your element. This is all part of the mindset you must adopt to make people like you more because you get to meet new people and develop new topics for conversation if you explore the world around you.

If you can't get out a lot, then at least delve deep into a hobby. That will help you meet others while giving you lots to talk about. No matter what the hobby, you are likely to find others who share it.

Say yes more than no. If someone invites you out, there is your chance to make new friends. Accept invitations and initiate yourself in new social situations. Even just catching up with old friends can help you relearn social skills and confidence.

Try to go out with someone, instead of alone. People are more drawn to you when you are with other people. This relates to the Principle of Likability proposed by Dr. Robert Cialdini [9]. The Principle of Likability states that people tend to like things that others like. So, if you appear in public with other friends, you are instantly more likable.

Take this example: You go to the bar to pick up chicks. No one talks to you. You seem like some creepy weird guy who is sleazing the girls at the bar. Then you take a buddy the next time and girls feel more comfortable talking to you. You have probably encountered this before and it's true of life: Having friends makes everything better and people talk to you when you are not alone.

Another key is to keep in touch with people. Once you meet someone, find out how to stay in contact, either through social media or in person. Exchanging contact information is a great way to start friendships and it is a more extroverted thing to do. The more you meet someone and talk to them, the more they like you. The result is a friendship born of mere exposure [10]. The mere exposure effect means that people like something the more they see it, so exposing people to your face is a good way to get them to like you. Most introverts don't want to bother people and don't reach out enough, so be persistent in reminding people that you exist.

Another extroverted thing to do is to talk to people as if they are already your friends. You don't need to get overly personal, asking questions and sharing things that are not appropriate. But speak to someone affectionately, ask them how they are, and keep track of things like birthdays. Remember details. These activities make people like you more and feel as if a friendship is already formed. Avoid being overly formal or bringing up how little you know each other. Instead, say things like, "How nice seeing you guys! Let's have a good time like last time."

Be like people who are extroverts. Watch how they stand in the center of groups or the center of the room and talk to everyone. Avoid finding a comfortable corner to hole up in, where you appear like a wallflower that no one wants to talk to. Don't just stick to one-on-one conversations all the time or stick to one friend. Try to talk to everyone. Introverts do better with one-on-one conversations, so you can make the rounds and meet everyone, having various one-on-one conversations. Don't just hold one and call it a night, or you just limited how many people you got to meet.

If you are an introvert, doing these things can drain you completely. You must avoid letting yourself get drained or you can become discouraged and give up on this personal work. The best bet is taking some time to yourself to recharge. Go to your house or favorite place to be alone and let yourself recharge on your own energy. That's what introverts are best at, being alone. You need some time on your own to clear your mind, organize your thoughts, and regain the energy to keep being extroverted. Go back out when you're ready. Try to make a habit of going out more. Over time, being extroverted will come naturally because your brain is used to it and no longer has to expend as much energy doing it.

Chapter 3: Finding Friends

You can learn social skills all day long, but what good do they do if you can't use them? Finding friends is easy enough in school, when you are surrounded by people you share at least a few things in common with such as age. But as an adult or in a new city, it can get a little more challenging to find friends. Finding them is still possible, however.

The Right Places To Find Friends

The right place to find friends depends on who you are and what you are looking for. A good starting place has to do with your particular interests and hobbies. You probably won't find a lot of friends in a church if you are an atheist. Hanging out with people who are diametrically opposed to your personality is not ideal, though you can certainly try it and see if you're surprised. Sometimes, trying new things exposes you to elements of your personality that you never knew existed. However, you usually know who you are, so stick to that and you will make friends who are like you. It is easier that way.

It is a safer bet finding something that you enjoy doing. Then you will naturally be at ease and other people will relate to you more. Look at a list of things you like to do or have always wanted to try and then find similar activities in your area. As long as you harbor interest in things, you will be more likely to project to others that you are having a good time, and that radiant positivity will draw people to you. There is nothing like a genuine smile to make people like you.

You should also look at things that you have always wanted to try but never have. Doing new things will expose you to new people and new opportunities. Always wanted to go sky diving? Do it! There is no reason to stay in your shell. Exiting your shell can be scary, but enlightening. You might never run into someone special or find out who you really are if you never try anything that scares you a little bit. Most shy people find extroverted activities, like improv, giving speeches, or going to mixers and business networking socials, very challenging. Since you are trying to become more social, it may be your best bet to visit some of these things and expand your horizons.

However, some activities are naturally more introverted. A community garden may be a place to make friends, but you're more likely to spend your time there alone. Try to pick out activities where you will meet new people, such as classes or workshops or even teams. If you are a crafter, go for a knitting club. If you are athletic, play an intramural sport. Do something that lets you meet others, rather than go off and be alone. The idea here is not to spend more time alone but to have opportunities to strike up conversations with strangers. The more people in an activity, the more likely you will find some new friends at it.

Try activities that you already have friends in. Having a friend can set you more at ease and help you seem more appealing to others [9]. Then you can make friends through your friend. Since you don't want to be a nuisance and cling to your one friend, you will feel pressure to expand your horizons and meet others. Take advantage of that. Be careful not to pigeonhole yourself with one group of people; try to talk to everyone present at the event or activity. That way, you can make new friends and be comfortable should your friend not arrive one time.

Social clubs are another good place to meet people. If you are a veteran, like volunteering, or want to play a role in your community, check out clubs for your interests. You might find a home at the VFW, Eagles, or Moose lodges. You might enjoy taking part in a Women's Club or the Boys and Girls Club.

Volunteering is a great place to meet people with similar interests and causes. Try volunteering at a place where you feel passionate about its cause. The shelter for animals, Habitat for Humanity for housing the homeless, the DA office for working with crime victims, and other such charities are out there. Often you can visit your local city hall for a list of local volunteer opportunities.

If you are religious, you can find a wealth of friends and support at a church, mosque, synagogue, temple, or prayer group. Trying new churches or temples can help you unlock your true spiritual calling. You will meet many people who are eager to get to know you and guide you on your spiritual journey.

Using Social Media/The Internet To Find Friends

In the Internet age, there is no better way to make connections. Social media allows you to meet people in a superficial way so that you can form a friendship. Then, when you meet, it's less awkward because you have already gotten to know each other a little bit and have things to talk about.

Chat rooms are a great place to meet people. You can find chat rooms for anything that you are interested in. Facebook groups and LinkedIn groups also let you find people with similarities to you and can help you grow your social and professional spheres. Finally, check out websites for organizations that you may be interested in joining.

Online dating is a nice way to meet new people, despite its bad reputation. Get to know each other for a while. Then go on a date in a public place and let someone know where you are going to stay safe. Dating sites that vet their members usually charge fees, but they are worth it.

Try Meetup to find local groups and activities. There are some meetups for every kind of hobby. Some meetups are just social clubs, where you can meet over coffee. The best thing about Meetup is that you can check out profiles of members of each meetup before going, to ascertain if you would fit in with this crowd. Meetup lets you try new things and meet new people. If you have never been to a floristry club, but you love arranging flowers, try it out. If you have never been bungee jumping, you can probably find a group that does that on here. If you want to learn a dance, you can probably find a club that does that dance and is eager to teach you.

If you have a specific interest, there is probably an online community for it. Online communities range from the ordinary to the bizarre, so find your niche. Even if you just like sharing funny cat photos, you will find people who love that too online.

Offering to help people learn English or learning a new language can help you network with people you never knew existed. There are a plethora of free language practice sites. You can tutor English or learn another language by receiving tutoring. This connects you with people from all over the world. Most of them are quite friendly.

Couchsurfing is a cool way to meet new people. It is an international network with chat and events. You can use it to find people in new areas to hang out with or even stay with for free. You can be a host and let people passing through your city stay in your home if you feel comfortable. If you don't, you can just meet people to hang out with or go to big Couchsurfing events. There is no obligation to ever meet in person or to host anyone.

The first key to social media networking involves building a winning profile. A lot of people lie on social media, but this makes it awkward when you try to meet people in person. Upload an accurate photo, fill out as much information as you can, and be truthful. Include photos of things you care about, like your artwork or your pets. Make this profile an extension of the real you. Try to find places to mention the coolest things about you, such as that time you went to Europe after college or your interest in model trains. The more you put on there, the more you prove to people that you are someone they would like to meet. Avoid mentioning overly personal or negative things, as this can deter new friends.

Be friendly and send people messages introducing yourself. A simple "Hi! I saw your profile and I think we could be friends" is sufficient. Stay on top of messages and reply to people in a timely manner. Try chatting about things you have in common and ask them lots of questions about what they are interested in.

Your online friends could be local people that you meet with in person. Or they could be long-distance friends. Those friendships can be just as fulfilling because you have someone to talk to. You can get to know people quite well online and see sides of them that they would never show in person. Some people claim that online friendships are not real, but if you get satisfaction from them, then that is the whole point.

How To Make Friends Spontaneously

To make friends spontaneously, you need to reach out to the people around you and put yourself in new situations. Reach out to neighbors, co-workers, and other people you have not previously talked to and try to find things in common to do. Go to new meet-ups or new places and talk to people.

To start a friendship, you want to find as much in common as possible. This increases your chances of having a common ground to start from. If you both like fly fishing, hey, there's a great place to start. You can invite this person to go fly fishing with you. That is just an example of one of the million things you can do to make friends.

In public places, comment on similarities with people. At a book shop, you can say, "I read that book. I highly recommend it." At a coffee shop, compliment someone's taste in beverage. Comment on someone's clothes with a nice compliment or comment on the music playing. Using environmental factors can help you find points of commonality with others. Stay observant to find things to talk about.

You can also listen to what someone is saying. If he or she is not locked in a private conversation, you are probably welcome to jump in with a comment that could kick off a connection. For instance, if you overhear someone telling the bartender about a local business closing, you can chime in with, "I heard that too. It's really sad! I used to go there all the time." That just ignited a new conversation.

Also, watch for clues. If someone says, "I have never been to that museum," propose that you go together.

If a person wants to try a new type of food, say, "Let's have a quest to find that cuisine!"

Center conversations around things you know. If someone is into books, talk about the books you know and ask them about the books they like. If someone wants to talk about current events, be sure to chime in. Politics and religion are often argument starters, so you may want to avoid such topics at first.

The more interesting things you come up with, the more likable you will be. If you find things to do that you both enjoy, your friendship can grow and become solidified. Try to make it action-based at first and then the more personal conversational aspect of the friendship will grow from there.

Making Friends In School/University

Schools and universities are full of opportunities to make friends. It is best to start in your classes and offer to help people study or propose study groups. Engage in conversation with your fellow students and find out who they are and what they like. If you talk to them enough, you might find things you want to do together, or you might get invited to a party. Don't be afraid to extend invitations to people to hang out.

Another great thing to do is to become involved in clubs and activities. Find something that interests you. not only do extracurriculars look great on your transcripts and resumes, but they help you broaden your horizons and meet new people you may have never met before.

Go to games and student meetings. Go to the library and smile at people. If there is a party, go. All these things make it easy to tap into the diverse population at your school.

Making Friends In A New City

Moving to a new city can make finding friends difficult. Without knowing anyone, you can't make the Principle of Likability work in your favor. Therefore, you must break the ice somehow.

The best way is, again, activities. You may also benefit from doing things at work, such as conventions, picnics, and office parties. When your co-workers go out for drinks, tag along. Say yes to as many opportunities as you can.

Many cities have social media groups for new people. You can make a post, "I'm new here and I want to know what I can do to make friends." Doing this will help you connect with other new people and by doing so, you can meet friends.

The other activities mentioned before work well, too. Find a hobby, get involved in a church, take part in a community endeavor, and/or volunteer. Take classes or join clubs. All these things can help you meet new people.

Often, it just takes one friend to get you out of your bubble. One friend can introduce you to a wealth of new people. Therefore, you want to work on finding that one person who is interested in being friends with you. Talking to lots of people and doing activities can open you up to a wealth of people, but just one person is often enough to get out there.

Feel free to ask new people you meet to show you the city. They can introduce you to new friends while showing you what a good time is in the new location. Don't be afraid to ask questions and ask to be introduced to new people.

Be Discerning

Most people who are shy are eager to make new friends. Therefore, they let their guards down and stumble into some very bad friendships. Predatory people can see your eagerness and take it as vulnerability. They will prey on you.

When meeting new people, it is essential to be discerning. You want to watch others. Consider this an audition, where you are not only making an impression, but you are deciding if other people are right for you.

There are many red flags to watch out for. If you spot one of them, don't pursue a friendship with that person. Dangerous people can pose as friends and then reveal their true colors later, but they often slip up and let you see one or two red flags immediately.

The first red flag involves people who are two-faced. She might be nice to you, but observe how she talks about other people in the room. If she smiles at someone and then turns around and speaks ill of him or her, that's a sign that she will speak ill of you too.

Avoid gossips. These people will do anything to get you to tell them secrets. Then they will tell everyone. They are not safe or trustworthy people. They will also twist things you say or make up stories. If someone is gossiping to you, don't feel like you're on the inside. Understand this person is a chronic gossip who will gossip about you when you leave the room.

People who tell even white lies are suspicious. They are likely pathological liars who embellish the truth to serve their needs. Once you catch someone in a lie, you should be wary. Everyone lies now and then, so you can forgive someone for a small lie, but you should proceed with caution. Chances are, this person will keep bending the truth to suit his or her needs.

People who must put you or others down generally have low self-esteem and can't celebrate the victories of others. These are the people who tell you, "Don't get a big head, dear" or "You got a promotion? There was one summer where I got five promotions! Back to back!" They either cut you down or find a way to one-up you. You will always find that you can't please these people and they will never cheer you on or encourage you.

Watch out for people who make you feel like you can tell them all. Often these people are manipulators who are adept at getting information out of you. The best bet is to be very private and reserved with your personal information until you get to know someone very well.

Also, watch out for people who many enemies. These people may play the victim and have great stories for why everyone hates them. But the truth is usually that someone with so many enemies deserves them. Listen to someone's reputation and proceed with caution. Chances are, people are right when they say "Watch out for that person!"

If someone constantly makes you feel bad, that's another red flag of a manipulative person. Say you're eating a potato salad and the person says, "I wish I could eat potato salad! You're so lucky that you don't have to watch your figure." You instantly feel bad about eating the salad. That's a sign that this person doesn't want anyone else to have what he or she can't have.

The friend who asks for a favor may not be a bad person. But watch out for future favors. You may find that this person is taking advantage of you. Be sure to set boundaries and put limits on how much you're willing to do for a person without getting anything back.

Obeying these warning signs helps you determine who is really your friend and who isn't. You can avoid or at least limit contact with those who appear to be toxic or unsafe friends. Always take your time to get to know someone.

Chapter 4: Starting Conversations

When meeting new people, all it takes one conversation to help form a friendship. A conversation enables you both to see if you should pursue the friendship or not. You obviously wouldn't want to continue a friendship with someone who talks about all her deep personal problems on the first meeting or someone who admits to enjoying torturing animals. A rude or cold person is also a deterrent. But if you both find things in common and like each other's personalities, a conversation is a gateway to a more profound connection.

First Contact – Body Language

Before you even open your mouth, your body language says a bunch of things that the other person can interpret loud and clear. From there, the conversation really hinges on your body language. The first impression you make in a conversation is always a silent one. Since at least 56% of your language is comprised of body language, 38% tone of voice, and the rest what you say, you need to be mindful of your body language to send the right message [11].

First, you want to focus on your facial expression. Facial expressions are universal, so people from all cultures will understand what your smile, frown, or grimace means. Smiling tends to get the most positive reaction from people; in other words, a smile can make someone want to talk to you [12]. For some reason, smiling also tends to make people judge you as more intelligent [12].

Some people "resting bitch face syndrome." This is not a real medical syndrome, but rather an anecdotal phenomenon. Basically, when your face is relaxed or in a neutral expression, it looks like you're angry. Resting bitch face syndrome can make people feel put off because they perceive you as angry and unapproachable when you're a really nice person. In social situations, plaster a smile on your face and don't let your face relax into a scowl.

Next, consider eye contact. Making eye contact shows a level of interest and comfort that can open a conversation [13]. But holding it too intensely for too long can be perceived as threatening. Try to avoid making too much eye contact; break eye contact every twenty seconds or so. However, looking away more than that can make you seem shifty or nervous, which is a deterrent [13]. Make eye contact first and smile and you have created a connection that may lead to a conversation.

Watch your stance. Being fidgety, slouched, or tense can convey that you are uncomfortable [13]. Being relaxed and holding your head high says that you are confident and ready to have social interactions [13]. Avoid crossing your arms and legs, as these things can seem like you are closing yourself off or being threatening [13]. Also avoid sticking your hands in your pockets, as this too can be taken as a sign that you have something to hide [13].

Different Ways Of Starting A Conversation

There are two main ways to start a conversation: risky and safe.

The safe way is easy enough. You make a comment about the weather or something pertaining to the conversation you want to start. You make an innocuous comment about the music, someone's clothes, or something else. These conversation starters won't offend anyone, but they can bore people. They are a great way to start when you are practicing.

Risky is a little more entertaining. This is where you catch someone by surprise. They include blatantly political comments, challenging someone to a game, teasing someone, a pick-up line, or even a joke that may be offensive. People may not respond – but if they do, they will be more interested in you than otherwise.

To start a conversation the risky way, you want to size up your conversation partner first. If you hear him making ribald jokes, for instance, you know he won't mind if you make one of your own. If she is wearing an anti-president shirt, you know how your views may match or clash with hers. Consider how the person looks, acts, and talks to determine how to best approach him or her.

Breaking The Ice

To break the ice, you might need to be the first to speak. People won't notice you or go out of their ways to talk to you in most cases. It falls on you to start the conversation.

If you are standing next to someone and an awkward

silence has ensued, it's time to break the ice. Say something to make a conversation happen. You can start practicing this on strangers in the elevator or with work colleagues to get comfortable with it. Remember, practice makes perfect!

A great ice breaker pertains to what is going on around you. Mention the game playing at a sports bar, someone's clothes, or someone's choice in appetizer. Making observations allows the other person to identify with you because you are both observing the same thing.

Another great one is to comment on current events. Most people are familiar with what is going on right now in the world. If they say they don't know what you're talking about, you can fill them in. They may ask questions and a conversation is born.

Yet another way to go about breaking the ice involves making some sort of joke. Most people like jokes. And if you make a funny one, you just intrigued that person. It may turn into an exchange of jokes.

Asking a person lots of questions about who they are and what they do is another way to break the ice. People prefer talking about themselves. When they meet someone who seems curious, they are eager to share. Look at a person's stance and clothes or office décor for clues about what they may be interested in. A lot of people leave clues about their personality everywhere to be found.

Finally, you can break the ice by mentioning something interesting about yourself. "I was in the army" could be a way to bond with another person who appears to be in the military or ex-military. Or "I used to work there" can start a conversation with someone who works at a certain place. Try to find something in common that you can gather about a person and then find what you can say to create that conversational bond.

Once you break the ice, the person has a choice to respond or not to respond. People who don't respond probably just don't feel like talking. Don't take it too personally. People who do may respond minimally, so you must keep the conversation going.

Remember And Say Names

When you meet a person, be sure to catch his or her name. Repeating this person's name multiple names can create a connection and cement a friendship [14]. In fact, experiment with this the next time a waiter serves you at a restaurant. Note his or her name and then use it whenever you ask for something. Notice how the server smiles and responds more genially. At the end of the meal, smile and thank your server and repeat his or her name. You will get excellent service this way.

Why does this happen? The brain activates a certain way when it hears its own name. There is considerably more activity within the middle frontal cortex, middle and superior temporal cortex, and cuneus when one's name is heard compared to the names of others [14].

When you do this in conversation, you make a person feel stimulated. You also excite the person's attention, creating a sort of attraction that is not sexual in nature. This attraction can make a person feel good around you, which causes him or her to want to keep talking to you. The person feels validated and heard if you use his or her name.

So, learn someone's name. Then repeat it often throughout the conversation. "Hey, Roger, so how is your job going?" "That's great, Roger. What is it that you do there?" Don't make it seem unnatural, just repeat the name a few times each conversation.

This goes on to repeating other facts and details you remember about someone. It can make people flood with dopamine and feel happy when you remember his or her birthday, for instance. Try to learn and remember as much as you can. Writing these things down in an address book can help you memorize them.

In future conversations, repeat things you learned about the person. "I remember you saying that you don't like Italian, Roger. Do you really want to go to that restaurant?" is an example of how you can sneak little details you remember into conversation in a natural way. Roger will be flattered that you bothered to remember his culinary preferences and a friendship is more likely to flower.

Continuing The Conversation

A lot of courses teach you how to start conversations. You may be a master at it by now. But what these courses fail to mention is how to keep it going. A conversation can quickly become dead in the water if you don't know how to keep it going.

Find Relevant Topics

When talking to someone, you want to find a relevant topic that you can both enjoy. A common interest is an excellent place to start. If you both love the same music, you can spend hours conversing about bands and songs that you both know. You can even show each other new songs. Finding that topic that takes up the bulk of your conversation is essentially finding the conversational sweet spot.

But it can take a few tries to find that sweet spot. You might have to bring up several topics. The way to find the sweet spot is to ask questions that start with who, what, where, when, and why. As you ask these, you can get more information from a person and learn what he or she may want to talk about.

You also need to be mindful of the other person's cues. If a person starts looking at exits, fidgeting, or checking their watch or phone a lot, you know that he or she is bored. It's time to switch topics. Bring up something new or ask a new question to renew the person's interest.

It's also OK to switch topics if you feel bored or uncomfortable. Except for some rude people who are totally blind to conversational cues, most people can tell when you're getting bored and restless. They may drop the conversation there. You can keep it going by proposing a new topic during the next lull in conversation.

Rapid conversational topic switches can throw someone off and cut off their thought process for a moment. Therefore, you want to stay more or less on topic. Just propose a new subtopic.

Topics Everyone Loves

Most people will be stimulated by the following topics and will have lots to say.

Family is one way to start and keep a conversation going. You might notice a picture of someone's child on his or her desk, so ask about the child. You will likely get some details that you can elaborate on. If you have a child too, you can find things to say to relate to the other person on. Or you might mention that you have no kids, but you want them one day. Family doesn't have to be about kids, either, as you can talk about any family members you find relevant to the conversation.

When you see someone, you haven't visited in a while, ask about how his or her family is doing. Listen and respond positively. Offer sympathy when the person mentions something sad or negative. Then mention your own family and things you two have in common.

Sports are another good topic. Not everyone loves sports, so if someone says, "I don't like sports," you know that's not the conversational sweet spot. But if someone does love sports, a conversation about it is likely to ensue. Ask them what their team is and mention how they played in the last game. Talk about your team and what you played in high school.

Music can get a lot of people talking. Ask someone what their taste in music is and compare. You can show each other new bands and songs if you have similar taste. Even if you have different taste, you can compare and contrast your favorite genres.

Culture is often a great conversation starter. Without appearing xenophobic, you can mention, "I haven't met too many [insert culture here]. Could you tell me more about it?" Asking people questions about their homelands, cuisine, and religion can really broaden your own knowledge and cultural sensitivity. Most people love talking about their cultures.

The same goes for travel. People love talking about

where they are from or where they have traveled. You should mention if you have been to the area they are talking about or haven't been there to determine where the conversation goes. You can talk about your experiences there or you can learn all about it from the person.

Work is a boring topic for some people, but everyone will tell you what they do and describe their jobs if you ask. Then, you can talk about your job. Commiserate on the things you hate, such as long hours, and chat about the things you do like. Focus on the positive more than the negative to avoid being a drag.

If someone has a pet, that's always a good source of conversation. Ask them about their pets and talk about your own. Even show them pictures. You will likely get some pictures in exchange. People love their pets and will enjoy talking about them.

If some catastrophe, severe weather, or major political event has happened, that can be a conversation piece. Mention, "Did you hear about that tornado?" While this is more of an ice breaker than anything, you can keep the conversation going by sharing a story about how you survived a tornado as a kid. Or mention how the weather is just getting worse every year. Current events can lead to a range of subtopics as you can touch on many things in the conversation. You can also learn some new things if the person you are talking to has some news or rich gossip you haven't heard.

Some topics are just banal. The weather is a good example. No one likes to spend hours talking about what a nice day it is. You can use the weather as an ice breaker, but then find something somewhat related to talk about to open a conversation. For instance, if you use the band playing at a bar as an ice breaker, you can switch the topic and keep the conversation going by talking about other bands you have heard. Don't just focus on that one band or the conversation can get boring fast.

Be Positive

I am sure you have had the unlucky experience of talking to someone who just complains and brings up negative things the whole time. It is not a fun conversation. You don't want to be that Debbie downer of you can pull the conversation down with you.

Being positive is good for conversation [15]. People tend to respond to positivity better than negativity. Don't start by saying, "I work at [insert company name] and I hate it. My boss is a drag." You should instead make light of it and joke about how you work more than you live, or something to that effect.

Point out the silver lining in every situation. That makes people feel good. Then they want to keep talking.

Don't Create Differences

How familiar does this sound?

Someone asks you, "Do you like fishing?"

"No, I hate being outdoors."

"Oh." The conversation ends there.

In this example, you just created a difference. That just made the conversation grind to a halt. You didn't attempt to find anything in common with the person. You just used negativity to shoot down their attempt at breaking the ice.

Many of us inadvertently create differences. But of course, we want to create similarities to spark similar neural responses that correspond to friendship [4]. That doesn't mean you should be fake and lie that you love fishing when you don't. You should just try a little harder to find something in common.

Back to the example, try this instead:

"Do you like fishing?"

"Not particularly. I'm not an outdoors person really. But I do like the taste of fish!"

The other person will probably laugh and talk about the great taste of some fish he caught last weekend. A conversation is born.

Use Dr. Cialdini's Principle Of Influence

In his book *Influence: The Psychology of Persuasion,* Dr. Robert Cialdini outlines six principles of influence that can make people do what you want [6]. These principles can easily be used to make people like you and keep a conversation going.

The first principle, reciprocity, is where you give someone to get something in return. This is the principle at play when you buy someone a drink at the bar and nine times out of ten, the person will come over to talk to you. Offer someone something small in exchange for conversation, such as offering to buy them a drink or bringing them a plate of food at a party.

The next one, commitment and consistency, is where people like their behavior to match their values. So, if someone cares deeply about something, you want to match that in your conversation. Talking to someone about what they would normally talk about makes them feel consistent and therefore good. It can keep the conversation going.

Social proof is where other people do what you are doing. So, if you wear a suit to a party, other people will wonder if they should have worn such a nice outfit. In conversation, you can make people copy you by starting the conversation on a certain topic.

Being an authority on some topic will make people gravitate to you because people love respecting authority. Using big words correctly and talking knowledgeably about something makes people want to listen. It can spark lots of conversation.

Social proof is where you get people to like you by already having other people like you. Having a friend at your side is a good way to get more people to talk to you. Otherwise, you can make people like you by giving them sincere compliments, smiling, and asking them questions about themselves. You don't have to have a friend at your side to make friends. It just makes things easier because friends can prove to others that you are a likable person.

Scarcity is where people feel that you are in limited supply, so they want to talk to you before someone else does. Being the sharpest looking person in the room, having the most unique things to talk about, and being kind can make clamber all over you. Then others will want to talk to you because you appear to be in short supply.

How To Win Friends And Influence People

Influence is a fantastic book about making people like you, but so is Dale Carnegie's famous *How to Make Friends and Influence People*. Carnegie describes some ways to get people to want to talk to you and to keep conversations going.

The main way Carnegie recommends you keep a conversation going is to be genuinely interested in other people. Instead of thinking about what you are going to say next, relax and focus on what the other person is saying. The other person will be able to see your interest and desire to talk. They will appreciate how you seem laser focused on their words and how you keep asking questions to find out more.

You want to make steady eye contact with breaks every twenty or so seconds. You also want to face the person and lean into him or her [13]. These things convey interest. As he or she talks, nod and offer the occasional affirmation to prove that you are listening. Ask questions related to what they say to learn more. When you speak, keep it on the same topic.

You should also smile a lot, according to Carnegie [16]. Carnegie understood how important smiling was without even knowing the brain chemistry behind it. Seeming enthusiastic, happy, and positive will keep the conversation going longer than being negative and pessimistic.

Focus on the person's interests and don't let your own crowd out the conversation. Keep talking about what the person wants to talk about. If it is a boring topic, find a way to make it interesting. Let the other person do the majority of the talking to make him feel as if you are truly fascinated.

Finally, make the person feel important. If your conversation partner mentions that he works in the meat packing department at a grocery store, don't downplay his job. Mention how important his job is. That will flatter him and make him keener on talking longer.

Ending The Conversation With A Great Impression

If you use Carnegie's tips, you should exit the conversation having made a great impression [16]. Simply making the person feel important and listening well makes you seem like an outstanding conversationalist. Nevertheless, there are still other things you can do to make this person walk away thinking, "What a great person! I want to see him/her again."

The first key to keep on top of your appearance. If you stink or have dandruff, you make a bad impression. You tell other people that you don't care about yourself, so how can you possibly care about them? You need to have basic hygiene down and you need to try to smell nice. Dressing in flattering clothes and wearing a flattering hairstyle is also essential. Looking like a dumpster when you have conversations will repel people.

Wearing red can help you make a good impression [17]. In several studies, women rated men wearing red as more attractive. A little red in your attire, such as red lipstick, a red hat, or a red tie, can make others find you more physically attractive. This physical attraction may not be sexual, but it plays a role in making people think that you are a great person. It is also a great job interview hack.

Try to be as tall as possible, which makes you appear

more confident and more assertive. People pay attention to taller individuals. Shoes can make you appear taller, as can clothes with vertical stripes. Holding your spine straight can add at least half an inch to your stature. Keeping your arms and legs uncrossed also gives the illusion that you are tall. If you are already a tall person naturally, you're in luck. People have more respect for you naturally. Otherwise, you have to fake it.

The second key is to making a good impression is to avoid being too nosy or personal. You don't want to ask, "So, how often do you shower?" or "Why did you get a divorce?" Most people will disclose things if they want to but asking will put people off. Maintain a polite level of distance in your conversation and don't pry. Good conversation involves asking lots of questions, but those questions are not supposed to be overly personal. It's not a good idea to pry into someone's personal life or ask about painful events. Touching on someone's health may be polite if they mention they saw a doctor or if you know they have an illness, but there are polite limits.

When you sense someone is getting uncomfortable, change the subject. Don't press on any issue that makes the other person avoid eye contact or start to fidget. If someone changes the subject, oblige him or her. You will make a bad impression if you press issues. Learn to drop things once someone asks you to or looks uncomfortable.

Also, don't be confrontational. If someone disagrees with you, don't start arguing. Don't push your opinion on a person. Simply accept your differences and move on in the conversation. Any sign of hostility or overbearing pushiness will make a terrible impression. This is not the time to be right and win. It is the time to make people like you.

Complaining a lot can also make a bad impression. You seem ungrateful if you complain about friends, family, and work. You also seem like a backstabber.

Avoid gossiping. This just makes you seem lower than you really are. Even if others are gossiping, politely excuse yourself from the conversations. Don't repeat what you hear or take part in silly squabbles. Don't offer opinions on arguments or fights that other people are having. None of that is any of your business.

You can be an expert, but don't be a know-it-all. Claiming that you know what you don't makes you look like a fool. Using big words incorrectly does not impress anyone. If you say something and someone proves you wrong, admit it with a smile and say, "Well, I stand corrected!"

There is a time and place for offensive jokes. You can share them with people who you know will enjoy them. Only dip to offensive or vulgar language and jokes if the other person does. For the most part, keep your conversation clean.

Practice good manners. This means holding the door open for people and saying please and thank you. Don't talk about vulgar or overly personal things and don't insult people or the host of an event you are attending. The wisdom "If you have nothing nice to say, don't say anything at all" is critical in making a good impression.

Using a person's name is critical. If you confuse people, be sure to apologize. No one likes hearing anything more than the sound of his or her name as you already know, so be sure to remember it well. Calling a person by the wrong name is very rude but it happens. As long as you apologize and correct yourself, you won't make a bad impression with a simple mistake.

Keep name dropping to a minimum. You can mention who you know to establish things in common with people. Don't use it as a way to impress people, though, or you just look arrogant. Definitely don't claim to know someone better than you do. People tend to do homework and they may find out that you lied.

Truthfulness is always the best way to make a good impression. If you lie to impress people, they may find out. Then they won't talk to you again and they will laugh at you behind your back. It is essential to stay honest. If you don't know something, say you don't know it. If you don't do something, admit it. There is no need to claim that you are someone you are not. You can still make friends being yourself – perhaps more so.

When you make promises, keep them. Follow up on things you said you would. Keep in touch and say hi later on. This proves to people that you are a person of your word. If you can't keep a promise, then don't make it. For instance, if you promise someone you meet that you will investigate a computer issue they are having, be sure to contact them later and offer to look at the computer again. Don't just blow it off or you look like a fickle person.

The final piece of advice is to give people the option to keep in touch. Give them your number or email or social media. Don't ask for theirs. That way, they feel more comfortable reaching out to you. If they don't want to talk again, they won't have to deal with the awkwardness of hearing from you.

Conversation Hacks

Everyone loves hacks. Things that make life easier are excellent, but hard to come up with on your own. Here are some ways to make conversations much easier.

Mirroring

Mirroring is the best conversation hack out there [18]. The simple art of mirroring enables you to create a bond out of thin air simply by mimicking the other person in subtle ways. Besides body language, it is one of the pillars of neurolinguistic programming, where you use body language and speech to trigger the responses you desire in the other person's mind [13].

Mirroring involves mimicking the other person [18]. Studies have shown that people respond really well to this and have more activity in the regions of the brain that correspond to relationships [18]. If someone smiles, you smile; if someone fidgets, you fidget. You watch someone and then carefully copy their movements.

It can get creepy if you are obvious about this. You want to leave a few seconds of a delay between mirroring. You also want to avoid staring at the person hard as you attempt to read their movements. It takes some practice.

Say someone is talking about her dog. She gets a sad

face as she mentions that she might have to put him down. Mimic this sad face. She will probably lean into you as she talks more about how she feels, so lean into her. If she lays her hands flat on the table, do the same. Mimic every part of her body language and she will feel more in tune with you, as if you really get her. She will enjoy this and will keep talking to you as a result.

Reflective Listening

Another hack is called reflective listening. Reflective listening is where you repeat back what someone says, confirming that you heard it [19]. You are not thinking about what you want to say or coming up with unsolicited advice; you are simply listening and proving that you heard every word.

It can be very tedious (and weird) to recite an entire paragraph that someone just said. Instead, you want to summarize the information from said paragraph and then reiterate the basics. The person will see that you were listening and will likely give you an affirmation that you heard correctly.

This is where you can practice becoming a bit of a therapist. As a person talks about something, you should nod in agreement, which really encourages them to keep talking. But then you want to reflect what they say. When they agree that you heard right, you can say something like, "That must have made you feel angry." The person will be invited to agree or disagree and thus talk more about his or her feelings.

Emulating a therapist in this way makes people feel good because it proves how invested you are in the conversation. You are listening, you are processing their emotions, and you are a sounding board.

By doing this, you are not inputting your own advice or opinions. This is a bad conversational habit that many people take part in. You are technically blocking communication by doing it. Instead, you want to be a sounding board. It makes the other person think solely about his or her problem, with no impediments to the conversation [19]. This is certainly refreshing and can lead to a new connection that is both strong and satisfying.

Open-Ended Questions

"Do you like volleyball?" you ask someone.

"No," the other person says.

This is an example of a close-ended question, one that can be answered with a yes or no. The conversation can basically die right there if you ask a close-ended question. Close-ended questions don't invite a person to partake in a discussion with you or disclose more information.

It is far better to ask open-ended questions, which require a person to think and deliver an answer beyond yes or no. Take the above example. "What sports are you into?" is a better question because it makes a person think and talk about the sports he or she likes.

When picking open-ended questions, focus on ones about the other person. That way you can invite them to talk about their lives and interests. People love talking about themselves and will prefer to talk about their lives instead of anything else.

Ask For Advice Or Help Of Some Kind

Another conversational hack is to make the other person feel useful. You can do this by appealing to their knowledge and expertise by asking for advice, help, or an explanation. People love proving their authority, so they will gladly share what they know to help you out.

It doesn't have to be a big favor. It can just be

something small like, "I know you're in securities and acquisitions. What can you tell me about this stock?" Find what the person knows a lot about based on what they do or talk about and then ask for advice or information.

Also, if someone mentions something that you know nothing about, feel free to say, "Tell me more," or "Can you explain that better?" That keeps the conversation going and educates you while showing that you are an interested listener.

Favors

Asking for favors can be helpful, too [9]. Known as the foot in the door technique, asking for a small favor can open a person up to doing more favors for you. Ask for something small and see how it leads to a friendship. You might ask someone to hold your coat, buy you a beer because you're out of cash, or something else tiny and unimposing. Later, you can give and ask more favors.

You can also do a favor for someone. This acts on reciprocity, where a person feels indebted to you and must return the favor [9]. Buy a friend a coffee the first time you hang out and he will likely buy you something down the road. Creating a give and take of favors is a good way to form a mutually beneficial friendship, as long as no one is taking advantage of the other.

Recognizing And Using Different Conversation Styles

Each person has a different conversation style. If you can communicate with someone on his or her preferred style, or find a person with your style, then you are more likely to communicate well without any misunderstandings. Most misunderstandings are simply things lost in translation between conversation styles. They can inhibit communication and make a friendship impossible to move forward, however, since communication and conversation are essential between human beings.

Nlp Sensory Modal Systems

A sensory modal system refers to how someone views the world around him and then communicates it to others [13]. Following the same sensory modal system of another person can help you understand each other better. The systems are based on the five basic senses: auditory, visual, tactile, taste, and smell.

Most people are visual. This means that they will talk about how things look and they will focus on colors and presentation. They tend to learn better from videos or visual presentations. When they speak, they say things like "Do you see what I mean?" or "Do you picture this like I do?"

When talking to these people, use more visual terms. Recognize the visual terms in their speech and match them. "Yes, I see this. But do you see what I'm saying?" If you match them on visual terms, then you will make more sense and they will feel more validated in what they are saying.

An auditory person talks more about what something sounds like or how something will sound. They use lots of terms relating to sound and they are audiophiles. They learn best by listening. They can often listen to something and remember it clearly. You will recognize this system by the way they say, "That sounds great!" and "How does that sound?" and "Do you hear what I'm saying?"

The other senses follow the same vein. Tactile people learn by hands-on and touching and talk about how things feel. Taste and smell systems are exceedingly rare but you will also be able to recognize them because that's all the person refers to.

Some people combine different sensory modal systems. If you hear someone combine two or more, then you can probably use whatever system is easiest for you. This person is a great communicator who employs all of his or her senses.

The Five Conversation Styles

Conversation styles also relate to how a person gets his point across. The main styles are assertive, aggressive, passive-aggressive, submissive, and manipulative [20]. People will generally use the same style in every conversation, but you may notice changes when they are addressing certain people. For instance, a person who is usually aggressive to his co-workers may become submissive in the boss's presence, out of deference to the boss.

- Assertive communication is generally considered the best because it is confident without hurting others [20]. Assertive people state their boundaries and goals but try to work with others to find a common interest. They make their own choices and take responsibility for them. They keep their body language open and relaxed, speak on an even keel, and have a normal volume and tone of voice. You will hear them say please and thank you.

- Aggressive is the opposite. These people often have low self-esteem, so they try to bully others and gain control. They are the ones seen standing in an intimidating way, yelling at people, or overpowering people with their voices. They are often rude and may insult others. They tend to stand too close to people and make eye contact for too long in order to gain dominance. These are the people who must get their way and win, no matter what.

- Passive-aggressive communicators are also rude, but not dominant. They tend to be sarcastic and devious, using jokes or snide remarks to hurt others and get their way. They can also be sulky or arrogant, depending on how others respond to them. They speak sweetly while their words are cruel. They stand in an asymmetrical way, such as with a hip cocked out, to show that they are not happy with how things are. Often, when someone leaves the room, they will start speaking badly about that person.

- Submissive people don't stand up for themselves. They avoid eye contact and keep to the corners. They stand with their bodies tense, their feet together, and their eyes down. They play the victim and say sorry too much. When they need to stand up for themselves, they usually can't. They let other people make decisions and have the floor when speaking.

- Manipulative people use emotions to manipulate others to get their way. They are often high-pitched and give compliments, only to follow them up with insults. An example might be, "What a nice haircut, Marge. It looks so much better than how you usually do your hair." They will sulk, pretend to be sad, or otherwise fake emotions. They are two-faced and bossy. Other people feel guilty around them and don't enjoy their company.

Out of these five styles, the best way to respond to any of them is to be assertive [20]. Keep an even body language and tone of voice. Smile, even if you don't like someone. Stand by your boundaries and say no politely, even to aggressive people who scare you. Don't play games with manipulators, ignore submissive communicators, get into fights with aggressive communicators, or let the sarcasm of passive-aggressive communicators get to you.

Being assertive shows that you have confidence and don't need anyone's approval. You are willing to stand up for yourself, which gains the respect of others. Refusing to play games or buy into someone's sulking can also make them respect you more. Always adopt this conversation style when talking to others for great results.

Question Askers, Open Sharers, And Ambi-Conversationalists

There is a final big conversation style difference: question askers and open sharers. This book has mostly focused on being the question asker. It has encouraged you to ask others questions to learn about them and find grounds to start a conversation on. There is nothing wrong with this, but some people take a drastically different approach.

In the open sharing approach, someone will talk about him- or herself. They volunteer information and answer questions without asking them. They sometimes make their life stories and sharing so interesting that others care and listen. Sometimes, they tend to overdo it, and make people get weary of the conversation. Open sharers tend to make conversations one-sided, all about themselves, which discourages others from participating.

To be a truly great conversationalist, you should be an ambi-conversationalist. This is where you ask questions *and* share information about yourself. You use both approaches to appeal to more people. First practice getting good at asking questions, as that's the easiest way to start conversations. Then practice inserting a bit of information about yourself or opening conversations with comments about your life, hoping that the other person relates and responds. You will find that a mix of the two approaches will actually make people enjoy talking to you more.

Different Cultures, Personalities, And People

Conversation is influenced by a huge variety of factors, which vary from person to person. Personalities, personal beliefs, and cultures can certainly influence how the conversation goes and how the person likes being talked to.

So far, this book has focused on how to make a great impression in the Western world. Being assertive, making good eye contact, firm handshakes, and smiling are all cornerstones of Western communication. They work on most people from American, European, and even some African cultures.

But Asian and Native American cultures are different. In these cultures, people don't like eye contact and consider a firm handshake an invasion of space. You don't ask personal questions and you swap a smile for a neutral facial expression.

Personalities can also be wildly different. You should observe a person to gather his or her personality before attempting to talk to him or her. You might be offensive if you tell a very conservative person a dirty joke, for instance, so watch for that.

The best thing to do is to go by what you know. If a person from a different background becomes offended, say you didn't know and ask, "How would you prefer that I act?" That leads to a conversation in itself. Plus, it makes you appear more culturally sensitive and you can let the other person guide you on how to be toward a certain culture or type of person. Be open to learning and you'll appeal to a broader group of people, which is very helpful in our global society.

The Internet can also help you learn these things. As you can meet a huge demographic of people online, you can learn more about their communication preferences. Talking to lots of cultural groups and religious groups online can help you learn how to speak to them in person. Be sure to ask questions when you feel confused or unsure and stay on neutral topics, or let the other person drive the conversation, until you get more comfortable.

How To Have More Substantial Conversations

A conversation can be boring and dull, focused on sports and the weather. Or it can be fantastic and enlightening, focused on substantial topics. Having more substantial conversations will be more entertaining and lead to more friendships. You don't want to just linger on banal topics; you want to find dynamic things to talk about that you both enjoy.

A substantial conversation can be philosophical, where you delve deep into questions about existence or how life works. But it can also be based on current events and true opinions. It can be about personal things, like how you feel or important stories from your past. It can even involve deep topics like how to fix our government or how to address life problems. A substantial conversation is about more than superficial topics and it touches both of you in profound ways.

Substantial conversations are not always possible. Some people just don't possess the intellect or depth to have such conversations. Some people repress their emotions so well that they don't know how to converse about them and take a conversation beyond the surface-level formalities. Therefore, you cannot expect to have a substantial conversation with everyone.

You can try the waters by posing an intellectual topic or question. See if the other person takes the bait. An intellectual person won't be able to resist discussing such a thing with you. People who can't keep up will get nervous or uncomfortable and not know how to respond. Then you know how to communicate with them and you can lower your expectations.

Also, speak to someone like your friend. This can open the gate to more substantial conversations. You can start by asking a personal question like, "What is your favorite memory?"

Feel free to disclose something about yourself. Something like, "I like stargazing because I gaze up at the stars and think about how they are all probably dead now, and I wonder what the sky really looks like in real time." Something like that will lead the other person to respond substantially. You must become comfortable with a little bit of self-disclosure to speak to someone like a true friend.

Avoid talking about negative subjects. You can have substantial conversations that are all bleak and you walk away depressed. If someone seems to be steering the conversation toward negative subjects, try steering them toward positive or pointing out the bright side. Otherwise, leave the conversation so you don't get down.

Usually, you will be able to tell if you can have a substantial conversation. It will just feel right, and such topics will come up naturally. You should never feel as if you must force it. Seek out people who like these conversations at events, bookshops, libraries, and other places where intelligent and deep people gather. You may just need one or two conversational partners to get your fix of substantial conversation. Don't expect to have truly meaningful talks at the bar or with party-hearty friends.

Chapter 5: What To Do After A Conversation?

Once a conversation ends, it could be the end of the whole interaction. Or it could be the beginning. The great things about conversations are that they can lead to infinite possibilities. But they can also be fickle and lead to nothing, even if they are wonderful conversations.

When a conversation ends, you can take certain actions to keep it going and make sure it doesn't just die. You want to make sure this person doesn't forget about you. Even if they don't contact you again, you can value the practice you got from this conversation and use it to develop confidence in having future ones that lead to more substantial relationships later.

Set A Point Of Future Contact

The first thing to do is to set up another future meeting. Don't just say good-bye. Say, "I'd love to meet again." Then hand the person your business card, phone number, or social media account. Mention another event coming up or some sort of thing that corresponds to the hobbies that other person loves.

Give it a few days and then call or text or send a request on social media. Make sure that you stay in touch. You may have to do the work initially. This hardly means that a person is not interested in you. It just means that he or she is busy.

Don't text or call constantly, or you will come off as a stalker. You want to be casual and wait a few days.

Better yet, let the person come to you. Give them a really good reason to call you and give them your number. Make sure communication is open. That way, the other person can decide about calling you or not.

Using The Mere Exposure Effect

The mere exposure effect means that someone likes you the more they see you [10]. At least five exposures can make someone like you; fifteen is best [10]. But the mere exposure effect seems to work even better when there is a lapse of time between exposures.

To illustrate this, there was a 1992 study where four women who looked similar attended a lecture [21]. They didn't talk or interact with anyone, they just sat in on the lecture and left afterward. One woman shown up never, one shown up five times, one shown up ten times, and one shown up fifteen times. At the end of the semester, students were asked to rate the attractiveness of all four women in photos laid side by side. Students rated the woman who had shown up to the lecture the most as the most attractive, even though she looked a lot like the other women. This just serves to illustrate how people will like you more the more they see you.

Once you run into someone a few times, you will already have more of a connection. Then, you will start talking more. Be patient and don't expect a friendship to erupt out of one conversation; it often takes many to generate a deeper connection than mere chitchat.

You can set up ways to run into someone several times. For instance, if they attend a business conference, they will probably attend others. You can even ask them if they plan on attending other conferences and then go to those.

It is also easier to make friends with people you have regular contact with for this very reason. Take your work colleagues. You see each other every day and that will lead to more of a connection. It will be easier to invite your colleagues out for drinks than a complete stranger. Attend events outside of work and you will get closer with your co-workers. Or consider attending block parties to get to know your neighbors better, or chat with your neighbors when you pass them or see them at the store.

Ask Them For Help

One way to ensure you see someone again is to ask for their help. If they mention that they design websites, ask them to look at yours and exchange contact info. If they mention that they are expert editors, ask them about how you can get your book edited.

Learn about someone by listening to them. Then find a clever way to compliment them and see them again in one swoop: ask them to use their expertise to help you. That makes it possible to see each other again in the future.

Send A Memorable Message

You met someone. Now you want to make a second impression. The best way to do that is to send a memorable message or email. You might want to reference something that happened when you met, making an inside joke to bond the two of you. Or you might try to refer to something that they told you. Ask a follow-up question. Possibly send a joke or follow up on something you told them about.

For instance, maybe you met someone by bumping into him with a drink and spilling it on him. Email him later asking if he got the stain out and make a joke about your clumsiness.

Or say you told someone that you are breaking up with your significant other. Now you can send a message asking how the person is doing. Add that you broke up. This invites future discussion.

Referring to something that happened or something

one of you said is the best to be memorable. You prove you were listening and paying attention, you refresh the person's memory about who you are, and you reaffirm the communication.

Send Them An Offer

Someone happened to mention that her plumbing is bad and she is looking for a new plumber. Do a little research to find a new plumber and send her the information. Letting her know that you were thinking about her and doing her a small favor can help her want to keep talking to you. It shows what a thoughtful person you are, great friend material.

Think of something the person mentioned wanting or needing. Then offer them that thing. This offer will almost guarantee a reply. It also acts on reciprocity and makes the person wants to do something for you [9].

Make Someone Feel Good

People will remember how you made them feel more than anything else. If someone remembers you making them feel good, they will want to feel good again, so they will keep talking to you. Trigger a flood of feel-good dopamine in someone by telling him or her a compliment after meeting.

A simple one is fine. "You looked really nice tonight" is good for someone whom you might want to date. "You performed so well" can spark a friendship. Make someone feel important, validated, and better about their insecurities, and you have hit the jackpot for future contact.

You don't want to make rude compliments. "You looked good despite your weight" is an example of something that might get you slapped. Find a compliment that is not offensive. Also, mean it. People can sense insincerity and an insincere compliment can really put someone off.

Chapter 6: Problems With Making Friends

You may feel discouraged that everyone seems to have friends but you. For some reason, your life or your personality just does not seem to be conducive to friendships. You feel lonely and isolated as you struggle to figure out why no one likes you and why you can't get out there and make friends. As humans are social creatures, this can be the worst feeling in the world.

The truth is that you are not alone. Many people face problems making friends. The difference between you and those other people is that you are doing something about it by reading this book. You can learn to navigate the common problems barring you from making friends and find solutions.

When Your Life Circumstances Interfere With Your Social Life

Various life circumstances can stop you from making friends. It's hard to make friends when you are always at work, you are isolated geographically, or you don't have money to go out. It can also be hard when you are in a new location or suffer from a disability or handicap that makes going out hard. If your significant other is jealous and prevents you from making friends, you are in a bad spot because you are enduring a type of abuse. Some people are psychologically barred from making friends, either because of severe social anxiety, PTSD, or other issues. A speech impediment can make it hard for you to talk to others because no one can understand you.

Navigating Disabilities

If you have some type of disability, you may find support groups or activities for people with like disabilities. There are activities like wheelchair basketball or autism support groups, for instance.

Often, you can go out and have just as much fun with a disability as others. It is only in your head if you think that you can't socialize or that people won't like you if you're disabled. Take your medications, use a walker or crutches or a wheelchair, and be yourself.

Speech therapy is ideal if you have a speech impediment or some other communication issue. Learn to read lips if you are deaf.

Some people who have been through trauma can't socialize out of fear. Soldiers with PTSD are a common example. You should attend regular therapy to learn how to cope with anxiety while in social situations. You should not let a mental disability or psychological one keep you isolated and trapped in the house.

The Internet can be a great asset for those with disabilities. You can find friends from the comfort of your home. You can also find support groups and chat rooms for people who suffer the same issues that you do. But don't let your disability make you think that you are not a viable friend. You can still go out and find plenty of people willing to be your friend.

Finding Time And Money

If you barely have time to eat and sleep on top of work, you won't have time to make friends. The best way around this is to set aside some time when you sacrifice sleep for socializing.

Often, people say they don't' have time after work, but the reality is that they just go home from work and collapse before the TV. They don't make time. If you make time, you will find it in your busy schedule. Put a big priority number one before socializing to make it part of your schedule.

Another key is to forget needing money to socialize.

You don't need to be rich to get out. There are plenty of free or cheap activities out there. Even if you go to a bar, you can get a cheap drink or water and sip on that as you socialize. There is no need to have money to go out.

Geographic Issues

If you live somewhere that is isolated, your best friend can be the Internet. You can find friends online and travel to meet them or invite them to visit you.

It may also be time to move. If your area is so isolated that you are unhappy, you should not endure it any longer. Being isolated can lead to depression [22]. People need human relationships and connections to feel happy.

Some areas may allow you to make friends, but there is not much to do. This is a common problem in small towns. It can be hard to make new friends when you know everyone and there is nothing local to do to make new friends. The solution is to either move, invent something to do with your friends, or visit activities and social centers in nearby towns.

When People Don't Seem Interested In Starting Friendships With You

A common problem people face when they start socializing is the sense that no one wants to start friendships. It is common to blame yourself and to think you are doing something wrong. You may be, but the issue may also be the people you are socializing with.

First, you must consider that maybe you are trying to enter the wrong group. Perhaps you have nothing in common with these people, so they are not interested in getting to know you. Perhaps they have all known each other since kindergarten and are too close-minded to allow a new friend. You can find a "Freeze effect" in some communities, where people are not interested in outsiders challenging their set routines and beliefs. By adulthood, you should have realized the universal truth that not everyone is friendly and nice.

In some communities, such as large cities, people have learned to be protective of themselves. If you are nice and chatting someone up on the subway, that person may assume you are trying to steal her purse. You can encounter a lot of unfriendliness in big cities, which is born out of a need to keep safe. Therefore, you should focus on meeting people through activities, where you look less suspicious than if you are talking to strangers in public places.

Second, consider that maybe your approach is wrong. If you appear too cold, shy, or submissive, you can make people feel uncomfortable because they are seeking confidence and assertiveness. If you don't smile enough, you may seem unfriendly. If you barely speak and don't volunteer any information about yourself, you end conversations before they can start and give people the sense that they can't get to know you.

You can't just greet people or say nothing at all and expect people to come to you. You must inject yourself into their worlds by drawing attention to yourself and going up to them. A greeting is not enough. You must actually try to make conversation.

You must ask people about themselves and show interest. If that doesn't seem to work, share something interesting or amusing about yourself. Remember, you must be an ambi-conversationalist, asking questions *and* disclosing bits about yourself.

Sometimes, the burden of inviting people out falls on you. You can chat all day and night, but the person still won't reach out. You must initiate the idea of going out. "Here's my number. Text me and I'll let you know when the next fishing derby is." That's an example of how you can find someone's interests and then act on it to hang out.

You may expect a friendship to bloom after one conversation. Or you jump in too quickly, inviting someone out after one meeting. The other person is still skeptical as he or she gets to know you. It is far better to extend an invitation, or expect one, after a few interactions, so that the mere exposure effect has set in. Remember, it takes a few exposures for people to feel sure about you.

Give it time and don't get discouraged after one setback. Perhaps someone rejected you or doesn't seem interested. That doesn't mean that you have failed altogether. Don't overgeneralize the situation and feel that you have failed in making friends. Just keep trying, with that person and with others.

Maybe people have invited you out and you've said

no. Now they have given up. You can fix that by apologizing and inviting them out now. Prove that you want to go out. Don't be flaky and expect people to keep trying.

You may also not make plans that fit the other person's interests or schedule. Ask some questions to find out what and when is best. Be sensitive to the other person. Making friends in adulthood often requires some careful negotiation, since everyone has work, school, kids, and other commitments. Don't give up. After a while, your schedules will magically work together on night and you get to hang out and take your friendship to the next stage. In the meantime, you can chat and get to know each other digitally through social media or texting.

When You Don't Have Friends At All

Earlier in this book, you learned that having a friend can help you make other friends through social proof

[9]. Obviously, this advice does more harm than good if you have no friends at all. How can you possibly get started?

Luckily for you, you don't have to have friends to make friends. You can strike out on your own and do well making new friends. The first key is to attend meetings or activities that interest you to put yourself out there. The second key is to actually talk to people, instead of expecting them to come to you. Seldom will people come to you, but they will appreciate it if you go up to them and try to strike up a conversation using the tips outlined in this book.

Quality Over Quantity

Truly popular people with billions of friends may be great people, but no one can have profoundly deep friendships with so many people. At least ninety percent of those friendships are likely to be surface ones with no depth. Therefore, don't feel bad if you don't have a huge friend group. One really good, loyal friend beats fifty thousand friends you barely know or care about.

Value quality over quantity. Get to know someone and be discerning. Only entertain the friends who make you feel good, who seem to actually like you, and who don't throw up red flags of danger.

Conclusion

Being able to walk up to a person, introduce yourself, and dive right into a conversation may be an art that has eluded you thus far. But with the science-based tips in this book, you should be more than ready to enter the realm of social confidence and comfort.

Being social does not mean that you have to alter your personality to become extroverted. You just have to start doing more extroverted things at times. That includes starting conversations and not being a wallflower at parties. Actually lead meetings and bring up ideas. Talk to people and ask them questions.

Talking to people is easy. You just have to find topics you both like talking about. Observing a person or asking them questions can help you find these topics. The sweet spot is the topic that makes a conversation go on for hours, without either of you getting bored.

It is also important to observe someone's conversational style. Use their sensory modal system and an assertive way of speaking when replying to people. This shows that you are confident, while avoiding misunderstandings.

Most people like confidence. Wearing red, having confident body language, maintaining eye contact, and speaking first are all ways to show your confidence. People will feel more comfortable around you and you will get more conversation and more friends as a result.

You should also use the advice of Dr. Robert Cialdini and Dale Carnegie. These wise men wrote great books about how to appeal to people. Using their knowledge can help you unlock many great friendships.

To make friends, you must leave your shell. You must get out and talk to people in new situations. Trying new activities or saying yes to invitations are good ways to get out there. Even if you have moved to a new city, it's more than possible to use the Internet to find new activities and friends, and even dates.

With something as great as conversation in your back pocket, you will find that life treats you better. As people like you, they will extend job opportunities, favors, and introductions to new friends. You can enter entirely new circles of people just by impressing one person. Be yourself and speak well, and you will make plenty of friends.

Making friends as an adult is not easy, or so people say. You can prove them wrong now. You have everything you need to start making friends and having great, even substantial, conversations. You just have to practice and put what you have learned here into action.

Stop being a wallflower. Actually walk into the center of the room and make yourself heard. People will come to you if you know how to talk and present yourself as a confident person. As you practice, you will get better and start to make more friends. With more friends, you will make yet more.

References

1   Daniel Campbell-Meiklejohn, Arndis Simonsen, Chris D. Frith and Nathaniel D. Daw. *Independent Neural Computation of Value from Other People's Confidence*. Journal of Neuroscience 18 January 2017, 37 (3) 673-684; DOI: https://doi.org/10.1523/JNEUROSCI.4490-15.2016

2   Longo, Michael. *Distortions of Perceived Volume and Length of Body*. ResearchGate. Cortex 111:74-86 DOI: 10.1016/j.cortex.2018.10.016.

3   Dr. Lawrence Michael Cameron. *Stinking Thinking: Think to Live Well Again. Taking on Maladaptive Cognitions and Dealing with Cognitive Distortions*. CreateSpace Independent Publishing Platform. ISBN-13: 978-1491047231.

4   Carolyn Parkinson, Adam M. Kleinbaum, & Thalia Wheatley. *Similar neural responses predict*

friendship. Journal of Nature Communications, Vol 9, Article # 332. 2018.

5   Facts and Statistics. (2019). *Anxiety and Depression Association of America.* https://adaa.org/about-adaa/press-room/facts-statistics

6   Gardner, B., Sheals, K., & McGowan, L. (2014). Putting habit into practice, and practice into habit: a process evaluation and exploration of the acceptability of a habit-based dietary behavior change intervention. Int J Behav Nutr Phys Act. 2014; 11: 135. doi: 10.1186/s12966-014-0135-7.

7   Carney, DR., Cuddy, A., & Yap, A. (2010). *Power Posing: Brief Nonverbal Displays Affect Neuroendocrine Levels and Risk Tolerance.* Psychological Science, Vol 1-6, DOI: 10.1177/0956797610383437

8   Renee Baron. *What Type Am I?* 1998. Penguin Books. ISBN-13: 978-0140269413

9   Cialdini, R. (2008). *Influence: The Psychology of Persuasion, 5ᵗʰ Ed.* Allyn and Bacon. ISBN-13: 9 78-0061241895

10 Yoshimoto, S. et al. (2014). *Pupil Response and the Subliminal Mere Exposure Effect.* PLOS One. 9(2): e90670. doi: 10.1371/journal.pone.0090670

11 Yaffe, Philip. *The 7% Rule: Fact, Fiction, or Misunderstanding.* Ubiquity. Volume 2011, Number October (2011), Pages 1-5. DOI: 10.1145/2043155.2043156.

12 O'Doherty, J., et al. *Beauty of a Smile: The Role of the Medial Orbitofrontal Cortex in Facial Attractiveness.* Neuropsychologica. 2003. Vol. 41, pp. 147-155. https://pure.mpg.de/rest/items

/item_2614428/component/file_2623264/conte
nt

13 Bandler, R., Roberti, A., & Fitzpatrick, O. (2013). *The Ultimate Introduction to NLP: How to Build A Successful Life.* HarperCollins. ISBN: 978-0007497416.

14 Carmody, Dennis & Lewis, Michael. *Brain Activation When Hearing One's Own and Others' Names.* Brain Res. 2006 Oct 20; 1116(1): 153–158.

15 Published online 2006 Sep 7. doi: 10.1016/j.brainres.2006.07.121

16 Lindquist, Kristen, et al. *The Brain Basis of Positive and Negative Affect: Evidence from a Meta-Analysis of the Human Neuroimaging Literature.* Cereb Cortex. 2016 May; 26(5): 1910–

1922. Published online 2015 Jan 28. doi: 10.1093/cercor/bhv001

17 Carnegie, Dale. *How to Win Friends and Influence People*. Pocket Books. 1998. ISBN-13: 978-0671027032.

18 Elliot, A. J., Tracy, J. L., Pazda, A. D., & Beall, A. T. (in press). *Red enhances women's attractiveness to men: First evidence suggesting universality.* Journal of Experimental Social Psychology.

19 Carr, E. & Winkielman, P. (2014). *When Mirroring is both Simple and Smart: How Mimicry can be Embodied, Adaptive, and Non-Representational.* Frontiers of Human Neuroscience. 8: 505.

20 Weger, Harry, et al. *The Relative Effectiveness of in Initial Interactions.* International Journal of Listening. Vol 28. Issue 1, https://doi.org/10.1080/10904018.2013.813234.

21 Newton, Claire. *The Five Conversation Skills.* Web. N.d. http://www.clairenewton.co.za/my-articles/the-five-communication-styles.html.

22 Moreland, Richard & Beach, Scott. *Exposure Effects in the Classroom: The Development of Affinity Among Students.* 1992. *JOURNAL OF EXPERIMENTAL SOCIAL PSYCHOLOGY, 28(3),* 255-276. http://dx.doi.org/10.1016/0022-1031(92)90055-O

23 Matthews, T. et al. *Social Isolation, Loneliness, and Depression in Young Adulthood: A Behavioral Genetic Analysis.* Social Psychiatry & Psychiatric Epidemiology. 2016. Vol 51, pp. 339-348. doi: 10.1007/s00127-016-1178-7

The Art Of People Skills

Little-Known But Powerful Social Skills No One Is Talking About To Improve Your Relationships Instantly

By

John Guzman

Introduction

You know how to talk. You even know how to talk to other people. Yet you aren't satisfied with how your conversations turn out. You want more depth, more friendships, and more quality to your verbal interactions.

A lot of people have trouble taking their conversations to the next level. Many of them inadvertently create hurdles with their words, and others just don't know how to get more depth or how to make people like them. To truly get the most out of conversations, you must learn how to listen effectively, handle people the right way, and avoid some of the biggest conversational mishaps that people commit.

As someone who was once awkward myself, I was stumped at how to make conversations turn into friendships and business leads. I thought I was doing well – after all, I said hi to people and was great at making jokes. Then I began to study the greats, such as Robert Cialdini, Robert Bandler, and Dale Carnegie. Under their tutelage, I became a master of conversations. Now my conversations can convert strangers into intimate friends with just one exchange. My business has thrived, and I finally got past the first date with an amazing person. All this success came simply from learning how to improve my conversations.

Everyone can benefit from improving their conversations. Many of us have habits or are stuck in ruts that prevent our success. Since conversation is the root of all social interactions, you absolutely must perfect your conversation skills. Then you will enjoy great success in romance, friendship, business, and even persuasion. Getting your way with other people and making people like you are as simple as learning how to speak people the right way.

With my research, I am able to teach you what you

need to know. I can show you simple tricks and rules that will turn your most banal conversations into enlightening and fun ones. This book contains everything you need to know about how to become a dynamic conversationalist, using methods proved by science.

This book is the answer to all your frustrating interactions, miscommunications, and missed opportunities. It will help you in every area of life as it shows you how to talk to people and elevate your relationships through words, listening, and body language. By the end of this book, I promise that you will have all of the tools necessary to expand your conversation skills from ordinary to extraordinary.

If you want to stop missing out on great relationships and driving people away with poor conversation, then you should get to reading now. If you want to grow your business and attract good clients or investors, begin Chapter 1 now. And if you want to learn how to get past that first date or make friends even if you are in a new city, don't delay reading. Your life will change for the best.

Chapter 1: Fundamental Techniques In Handling People

You may not realize that your conversations are way more than words. They create the dominant-submissive power play, they set the relationship dynamics, and they form the opinion the other person has about you. They are incredibly important to each relationship you have.

Therefore, you must learn how to use them to your advantage. Basically, learn how to handle people through conversation. That is what this book is all about. To handle people correctly, you must employ some simple yet crucial rules to your conversations. Neglecting to follow these rules can lead to various bad things, such as not being taken seriously by the other person, losing likability or credibility, or even making a person hate you or distrust you.

The 3 Big Don'ts

In conversation, there are three basic don'ts's: don't criticize, condemn, or complain. These three things can kill a conversation or make it turn unpleasant very rapidly. Avoiding these habits will make your conversations richer and pleasanter.

The truth is that most people do these things as if by instinct. They are inadvertently hurting conversations. Chances are, you engage in these habits yourself. To have better conversations and improve your social skills, it is best to avoid doing all three.

When you criticize, you make people feel uncomfortable or even angry. Many people don't mean to criticize. But here are some examples of criticism that can create a conversational rift that halts any future relationship:

"This music sucks! I wish they'd play something else."

"You wear a lot of red. It looks good on you, but I hate red."

"You could have done that differently. Here's how I would have done it."

See how these things don't seem hurtful outright? Yet they really are criticism. They put down another person's actions, views, or preferences. This can make a person feel injured or even angry.

People respond to criticism in a very negative way. In a study, adolescent girls were exposed to audio clips of their moms speaking praise, critical, and neutral phrases while undergoing MRI scans [1]. All the girls had greater activity associated with anxiety in the amygdala when hearing criticism; they released oxytocin in the brain when they heard praise [1]. The study also found that girls who heard more criticism while growing up tended to have more depression and anxiety, stemming from activity in the amygdala [1]. It appears that listening to lots of criticism while growing up can permanently hurt a person's brain, making that person engage in negative self-talk and self-criticism.

Therefore, bear in mind that speaking critically actually hurts a person's brain. Use more praise when you speak to others. The results will be more positive.

The same goes for condemnation. Not unlike criticism, condemning people or things is a harsh form of criticism that lets people know you don't approve of something they like or do. It acts much like criticism and is not healthy for the growth of relationships.

Complaining makes you appear to be a negative person. A lot of people tend to complain in conversations, hoping to commiserate with the other person. Complaining feels good, as it lets you vent and get things off your chest. You may notice that this works at times, such as when you comment on the horrible weather and someone else agrees. But have you also noticed that the conversation usually stops right there, unless you change the subject to something more positive? Complaining starts the conversation on a sour note. It rewires the brain for negativity, leading to more negative conversations [2].

Most people complain for one whole minute in a conversation [2]. The way to break this habit is to set a purpose for the conversation, so you don't resort to a habit like complaining out of lack of better things to say. Then start with something positive – a pleasant compliment, a nice comment about the weather, or something else that is happy. You can even mention your complaint but mention a silver lining to it, such as, "This rain is cold, but it's so good for the earth right now. We needed it!" Also, if you do complain, keep it focused on the issue at hand and then move on. Don't dwell on your misery for an hour. Be sure to end the conversation on a positive note, as well, so the other person walks away feeling better about the whole conversation.

Give Honest And Sincere Appreciation

You already learned that praise releases oxytocin in the brain, which is a hormone that leads to attachment and fondness [1]. In fact, oxytocin is the chemical that makes mothers bond with their babies and couples bond after having an orgasm. Therefore, littering your conversation with praise that you actually mean is a great way to make the other person feel closer to you.

One way to praise people is to give honest and sincere appreciation. You compliment how well a person is doing at their job, or how well they are dressed, or how good they make you feel. You offer some sort of positive feedback that you actually mean.

Sincerity and honesty are both key here. The reason why is that people tend to sense insincerity. If you are just flattering someone without meaning it, they will be able to tell [3]. Then the praise falls flat and the person think you are just a brown noser! People can feel when you mean your flattery and it makes them feel good.

When you flatter someone, they not only get a rush of oxytocin, but they also become more sensitive to praise in the future [3]. This means that they keep looking for praise, almost like they get addicted to it. This creates a lasting bond and acts as a fantastic motivator, even more effective than guilt or fear [3].

Arouse In The Person An Eager Want

People only do things when they have a buy-in. They must perceive that talking to you is worth their valuable time. This is especially true in business or romance, when you must convince the other person that you are worthy of their attention and continued participation. The only way to do this is to arouse in the person an eager want to get to know you and keep talking to you.

While future chapters delve more into this, the basic principle at play is finding what a person is interested in. Then offer that to the person through conversation. Finding things in common can help here. Having information that this person wants can also help. If you appear to be an authority or a good influence with lots of friends, the other person will want to get to know you as a part of social proof [4]. Finally, just providing someone with the attention and praise they crave gives him or her the buy-in [3].

Chapter 2: Ways To Make People Like You

There is no guaranteed way to make someone like you. Some people just don't have anything in common with you or are predisposed to dislike you. Sometimes egos clash and people don't get along. Generally, however, you can make people like you by employing some techniques from Dale Carnegie's legendary book *How to Win Friends and Influence People* [5]. The techniques in this book provide a handbook for how to relate people and warm them up to you, so that your conversations can turn into friendships or more. Using these techniques will probably earn you many friends – or at least help you avoid making enemies.

Become Genuinely Interested In Other People

If you pretend to care about people but don't really care in your heart, it shows in subtle ways. You might look around the room, betraying your boredom. You might have to suppress a yawn. You might even angle your feet toward the door in a subconscious desire to leave the conversation. Other people are startingly sensitive to body language, whether you realize it or not, and they can tell when you don't really harbor interest in them. Most people will eventually close the conversation and move on to someone who does care. The relationship ends there.

But if you make yourself actually care, then you show it as well. You lean toward the person and make eye contact as you listen. You ask appropriate questions and bring up relevant new subjects. Everything about your speech and body language shows that you want to be right where you are, taking part in this conversation.

To have more meaningful connections and improve your conversation, spark a desire about others within yourself. Find reasons to care about what they have to say and express it.

You might have to search for reasons. Listening to someone talk about something you have no interest in can be difficult. A simple desire to learn new things can help you express interest in subjects you never cared about before, though.

Interest in what someone is saying is not only respectful, but it is a form of praise. You already know how important praise is. Providing praise in the form of making a person feel important by listening well gives the person the buy-in needed to keep talking to you.

Remember, A Person's Name Is The Sweetest Sound In The Language

Learn a person's name at the beginning of the conversation and then repeat it often. The truth is that people react strongly when they hear their own names, showing a preference to that stimulus [6]. Research has shown that people really do find their own names to be the sweetest sounds in the language. Activation in the middle frontal cortex, middle and superior temporal cortex, and cuneus show that names recall self-representational behavior and trigger a major neural response [6]. Brain science aside, you can see this in action when you say someone's name: They perk up and respond to what you have to say next.

Try it the next time you are out at a restaurant. Notice your server's name and then use it as you order. Your server will likely perk up and smile and respond to you in a more personable fashion. The connection that occurs when you use someone's name often in conversation creates a greater connection.

It also proves that you listen and you care about that person as a human being. You are not just talking to a stranger. You are talking to Margaret, or Cathy, or Tom. This makes a person feel better about talking to you, as if he or she is being valued and heard.

Talk In Terms Of The Other Person's Interest

Giving people a buy-in to talk to you is as simple as talking in terms of the other person's interest. You won't appeal to the person as much if you are going on and on about yourself or the things only you care about. Taking the time to find out what someone likes and then appealing to those interests will make you a better conversationalist.

Think back to a one-sided conversation you had with someone. It was pretty boring, wasn't it? As the person went on for hours about what she likes or what he ate yesterday, while never asking you about yourself or talking to you about anything you like, you started to feel like a zombie. But you may inadvertently do the same things while talking to others. As you focus on things the other person doesn't care about, you bore that person. They are eager to get away, and there is no eager want to keep talking to you.

Throughout the conversation, you want to make the other person feel as if this conversation is worth his or her time. Letting the person talk about his interests, teaching the person something he is interested in learning, or comparing notes with a fellow authority on a subject you both know a lot about can make a conversation fit in line with someone's motives.

When it comes to business, your conversations should be succinct and to the point. You want to show the other busy person why you want to talk and what he or she can gain from the conversation. From the beginning, make it clear that you have a winning proposal or that you have some information the other person might want.

You may also find lots of things in common when you cater to someone's interest. When you find out someone's interests, you can match them with your own. That gives you both more to talk about. Plus, it creates a bond, since people tend to make friends with those who share their neural responses [7]. If you both get excited about the same things, that shows a mirror in neural excitement that leads to a friendship. Then the bond is stronger and the conversation is more enriching.

Start by asking the person lots of questions about what he or she does, what he or she likes to do for fun, and the like. These questions help you find topics that you can both enjoy talking about. You may also look at the person or his/her surroundings for clues. A shirt or baseball cap can indicate the person's interests and you can ask about it. Ask about the books the person is reading or has read, or the movies he or she likes to watch. Ask their opinions on different things, such as current events.

Make The Other Person Feel Important – And Do It Sincerely

"Hey, that was a great speech. I really appreciated your views on the campaign." This is an example of an excellent way to start a conversation that makes a person feel important.

Making a person feel important is key to giving him or her the buy-in to talk to you. It is a form of praise that makes a person feel both motivated and eager to talk to you. As long as you mean what you say, your positive feedback can make the person want to keep coming back for more [3].

Most people are riddled with insecurities, even if they hide those insecurities well. When you make a person feel affirmed as an important person in the lives of others, you validate that person's need to feel like a valuable part of the world. In Maslow's Hierarchy of Needs, the need to feel loved and the need to have a sense of belonging sits at the middle, right above basic safety and physical needs for survival [8]. That means a person really needs this! The need to be esteemed is above that, and at the pinnacle of the pyramid sits the need to be self-actualized, which means to be using one's full potential [8]. Making someone feel important can appeal to those two needs as well, as it confirms that a person is both esteemed by others and using his or her potential to thrive in life.

Maslow's Hierarchy of Needs provides a visual representation of goals that motivate most people [8]. Therefore, by playing to those needs, you can motivate someone to take an interest in you. Appealing to the top three through validation of a person's importance is significant.

The best time to make someone feel important is when they don't. When a person appears nervous, down, or doubtful, you can give him or her that little boost of self-esteem with this form of praise. Then you really appeal to the person's need to feel important because you gave it when the person didn't feel important. Praise a colleague after a hard speech, or an artist after a show or performance. Praise someone who has worked hard, only to be criticized by the team or the boss. Praise your partner for being there for you and being instrumental in your life. Praise your friends for making your life better and show them that you value their roles in your existence. Tell a stranger that he seems to be doing a good job or that you value his contributions to something.

Have you ever considered making your trash guy or your server feel important? These people make your lifestyle possible and comfortable, yet few of them receive any recognition for the importance of their work. An unexpected friendship may arise if you praise the people in your life or the strangers you encounter that you think of the least.

Chapter 3: How To Win People Over To Your Way Of Thinking

A difference in opinion or viewpoint can make any conversation tricky. Plus, it can impede your progress in life. To be truly successful, you must be able to persuade people to see things from your point of view and give you the permission or affirmation you need to move forward.

A good example is getting your boss to see why you should get nights off or getting your project leader to see why the project will be better if he allows you to move in a certain direction with it. Another example is convincing a new friend to go to a certain place to eat or getting people to vote for your candidate or even to get people to donate to your cause.

You can't get people to say yes to you if you don't get them to see how they will benefit. The key to getting people to see your point of view and agree with you is motivating them. Finding motivation can be achieved with the following methods.

Begin In A Friendly Way

Many people intend to have a friendly conversation. Yet when a difference of opinion enters the picture, they get confrontational and raise their voices. They often don't mean to. Excitement and passion get the best of them.

But you must realize that doing this only creates a conversational barrier that prevents the person from ever wanting to see your side. As you begin to argue and yell, you put this person on the defensive. Defensiveness occurs when a person makes emotional maneuvers to avoid taking responsibility for an act or feeling something unwanted [9]. Once a person becomes defensive, there is no hope going forward! The other person is too busy trying to deflect conflict or blame to listen to you. You either start an ongoing argument or you convince this person entirely to never take your side. The conversation will end on a very unpleasant note.

When people get defensive, they tend to become blind to facts and reason [9]. All they want now is to defend themselves and win. They feel threatened and attacked, which is never a pleasant feeling for anyone. People will do anything to thwart this feeling, including resorting to threats or manipulation [9]. They will go to great lengths to preserve their ego and restore their sense of right. You want to be sure never to prod someone into a defensive mood.

To get a person to come around to your point of view, you must start in a friendly and respectful manner. Start with a warm greeting and an invitation to speak about something. Ask the person, "If this is a good time for you, I'd like to address [insert topic or issue]." By asking for permission to proceed, you can make this person feel important and respected.

Perhaps the difference of opinion occurs while you

are speaking. In that case, you are not beginning the conversation, but simply changing its purpose. The key here is to say, "I think we have a difference in opinion. I'd like to hear your thoughts before I share mine." This respectful way of beginning the conversation change helps to avoid an argument.

Use lots of "we" terms. This means that you say things to create cohesion as a team. "We can really make great strides if we do this!" Using "we" terms can make a person feel as if you are in this together. Then they will soften more toward your way of thinking. Insert "we" whenever you can. You will lose a person's attention and motivation if you simply speak about yourself and use lots of "I" terms.

You should never be confrontational or make an accusation to begin a conversation. Otherwise, you just started the whole discussion off on the wrong foot. You put the other person on the defensive immediately. The key is to invite this person to participate in a talk, not anything else.

Avoid saying things like, "Because of you, this happened" or "People like you are ruining our country!" Accusing someone puts them on the defensive, plus it divides the two of you. There is no hope of creating unity and harmony with that division in place.

Instead, use vague terms. Don't refer directly to the person you are speaking to. For instance, you might say, "Democrats as a whole seem to vote this way. I feel that we should vote this way instead. We can get more done that way." That is better than saying, "You vote like this. I think that's the wrong way to do it."

Keep a smile on your face. People respond well to smiling [10]. Seeing a smile activates the medial orbitofrontal cortex and stimulates the release of both dopamine and oxytocin, feel-good neurochemicals. As you smile, you keep the other person feeling happier and more at ease. You avoid letting the person feel bad, which can make the conversation turn from friendly to unfriendly.

Also, keep your voice down. As people speak about things they are passionate about, a spike in volume is only natural. The other person is only going to respond to that by becoming defensive and loud himself. You can avoid that by keeping your voice level. This may require some restraint, but it is how you keep the conversation friendly. Feel free to take a moment to regain your composure if you begin to feel like you are going to raise your voice.

If you are trying to convince someone to honor a request, these rules apply, but you should also appeal to the person's importance. Make them feel in control and dominant. This way, you flatter their egos. They are more inclined to give you what they want just to prove that they have the power to do so. It's a great way to put in a request with your boss, for instance.

Respect The Person's Opinion

You might disagree with someone, or even hate what he or she has to say. This doesn't mean that you should tell the person how much you disagree. Understand that respecting someone's opinion is critical.

People value their opinions highly. Opinions are the framework that shapes a person's world [11]. In fact, personality traits and beliefs that are taught help shape someone's opinions [11]. A high level of the personality trait essentialism, where people believe that each group has essential characteristics that separate them, can lead to people supporting segregation of different groups, such as men and women, straights and gays, or other such groups. Therefore, opinions are often facets of one's personality, rather than mere ideas that a person holds [11].

This is why people treat their opinions as facts, no matter how wrong their opinions may be compared to reality. Opinions are born of someone's background, experience, and personal values. A person forms them over time and holds them sacred as a result. Disrespecting someone's opinion is the same as disrespecting the person. If you disrespect someone's opinion, you will get a lot of defensiveness as a result.

To respect someone's opinion, start by acknowledging it. "I understand that you think that way" is a good and simple thing to say in order to accomplish this feat. You want to prove that you heard and understood the opinion. Otherwise, the person may feel as if you didn't get it and will keep explaining himself or herself, at a loss that you might just disagree.

Next, point out why you think that person may hold that belief, or how it is valid given the circumstances.

You want to show that you really understand why a person may hold an opinion unlike yours. Doing this validates the person, instead of attacking him or her. It leads to a healthy discussion because you are being so respectful. The other person will let his or her guard down, since you are not attacking.

Be sure to point out the positives in one's views. Even if you don't agree, a silver lining can be found if you look hard enough. Pointing out these positives can help you make the person feel understood better.

It is even possible to agree to disagree. What will you gain by making this person see things your way? When it comes to a matter of personal politics, religion, or some similar topic, people have a right to hold different viewpoints. It is possible that no one is right or wrong. While people hate to admit it and prefer to prove how right they are, the truth is that nothing is that simple.

Walking away from an argument is the only way to win one [5]. Therefore, it may be better to simply agree to disagree with someone than engage in a debate that will never end. If someone is being confrontational, rude, or argumentative, you can shut the argument down by simply smiling and saying, "I can see we don't agree and that's OK. I hope you have a great day." Then walk away. You don't need to tolerate that. You certainly won't win with such a person.

Nevertheless, you can avoid having someone do this to you by simply being respectful. Don't just argue or make accusations. Don't push your agenda and tell the person that you are right. The key here is to be respectful so that the person feels comfortable continuing the conversation. It can be very engaging and enlightening to discuss differences of opinion with someone in a respectful, tolerant manner. You can learn some new things and teach some new things.

In the future, if you agree to disagree with someone, you should take the person's views into consideration. If your sister-in-law is a vegetarian, don't insult her by making steak whenever she comes over for dinner and offering no alternatives for her to eat. If your co-worker is Muslim, treat his religious beliefs as sacred and respect them. If someone you know is a Republican and you are anti-Republican, don't just talk about how much you hate the president every time he or she is around. Take someone's opinions into consideration and treat them respectfully at all future interactions. It will make the person like and respect you so much more.

Avoid talking about points of difference with the people you disagree with. Instead, talk about what you do have in common. This is also a sign of respect, proving that people of different groups and mindsets can get along. It can help you stay friends with people by finding similarities to bond you, instead of differences to divide you.

Always remember to compliment someone and make them feel important, even if you disagree with them. Make it clear that your respect and affection is not diminished by a difference in opinion. If you do this during a conversation, then you will never make an enemy. This does not mean that you ever have to pretend to agree with someone or fake who you are; you just need to continue to show that you like them.

If You Are Wrong, Admit It Quickly And Emphatically

On a long enough timeline, everyone is proved wrong at some point. Everyone makes mistakes and everyone forms wrong opinions. Being a good person partially involves recognizing and admitting when you are wrong in light of facts. Being stubborn and refusing to admit that you are wrong will simply make other people dislike you. If you do this, you look bull-headed and even foolish.

Have you ever had a friend who couldn't be wrong? Or a boss like Michael Scott on *The Office,* who tries to cover up his mistakes and looks like a fool? Then you know what it looks like to do this yourself. Yet so many people make the mistake of refusing to admit when they are wrong out of pride. No one wants to admit to having the weakness of being wrong sometimes, but everyone is wrong at some point, so you can't pretend to be perfect forever.

It takes a lot of courage to admit that you are wrong. When you are wrong, it is an ego blow that hurts a bit. You may worry that you look stupid to other people. But you can save face by simply admitting your mistake and learning from it. You want to do this as soon as possible and correct the wrong instead of pushing forward. People will respect you as a result.

Plus, this plays into the reciprocity principle,

proposed by Dr. Robert Cialdini [4]. If you admit that you are wrong, then other people are more likely to admit to wrongdoing in the future too. They do this out of a need to do unto you as you do unto them, or to return the favor [4]. Reciprocity allows you to model the behavior of others by doing things like favors that you expect them to return eventually.

How do you go about admitting that you are wrong? It is important not to make a big deal out of it. Simply say, "I am sorry, I was mistaken." You may point out what you have learned and what you have gained by correcting yourself, as well. You may even illuminate why you realized that you are wrong. But you don't need to apologize over and over.

Make apologies personal. If you said or did something wrong to a person, apologize to that person directly and say, "I am sorry that I hurt you in this way. I see what I did wrong now." If you were wrong about an opinion or fact in conversation, bring it up when you see the person next and say, "I would like a chance to correct something I said wrongly last time we spoke."

A public apology is another gesture of confidence and courage if you have done something wrong that a whole group of people knows about. You may stand up before the office, for instance, and declare that you have discovered an error in your judgment and you want to correct it. Ask people to please allow you to correct yourself. By asking their permission, you appear more respectful and courteous.

Own up to things you do or say wrong to your boss, partner, or another important person in your life. You can avoid a lot of fights if you do this. Speak to the person privately and personally. Mention that you were wrong and would like to apologize. Ask the person for a chance to correct what you are wrong about.

After you apologize, wait a moment to give the other person a chance to speak his or her mind. Let the other person express any feelings he or she may have. People prefer a chance to express themselves, instead of having to bury their emotions and then letting them fester over time. If people are angry, simply say that you are sorry for their anger. If people are hurt, apologize once again for the damage you caused. Take full responsibility but don't try to dismiss someone's feelings. Invite the person to work on a solution to the disagreement with you now. Use those "we" terms to invite collaboration together.

Emphatic means to do something forcibly and with clarity and passion. Therefore, make your apology concise, to the point, and clear. Don't mince words or delve into a flowery speech. Also, don't try to shirk responsibility by avoiding a direct apology and admission of what you were wrong about. Be very direct and don't take too long in your apology. You will earn even more respect if you don't waste people's time.

Furthermore, there is no need to keep apologizing or bringing your mistake up. Allow yourself and others to move on. Change the subject once you have apologized and the other person has spoken his or her mind, to begin a new vein of conversation. Or begin collaborating together toward a solution to the disagreement.

Never Say "You're Wrong"

The single most harmful words in the English language may be "You're wrong." When you say that, you put a person on the defensive automatically. You also dismiss any correctness or reason that the person may have for his or her opinion. "You're wrong" creates a huge communication roadblock that can really screw up any chance of a future collaboration.

Try Honestly To See Things From The Other Person's Point Of View

You want a day off to see the Mets game. Your boss wants to meet a deadline to avoid more pressure from some high-profile clients. As you argue for your day off, you will run into some issues if you don't try to see your boss's dilemma and desire for you to work that particular day.

If you can read why someone is doing something, then you can figure out how to offer them what they want in exchange for what you want. You might offer to work an extra day on the weekend, for example, in order to get a particular day off with your harried boss.

Just like with opinions, people hold tightly onto their points of view. They believe they are right, and in many cases, they are. This does not make you wrong. You just need to appeal to them and show why their point of view does not need to clash with your own.

The only way to figure out how to do this is to see things through their eyes.

Typically, empathy is sufficient for understanding why a person sees things a certain way. Consider that person's position and background. Think about how your idea may go against what he or she wants. If you are trying to sell a car, for instance, you need to consider someone's point of view regarding money and the necessity of certain features. Only then can you appeal to the person's wants. A mom with three kids may have a very different point of view about what car she wants than a single guy in college trying to impress girls.

Sometimes, seeing things from someone's point of view is not easy. In these cases, you should ask the person more information. You can say something simple like, "Could you explain to me why you feel that way?" Asking for feedback helps you realize and address the person's concerns.

Never assume that you know what someone else thinks. Assumptions may be wrong and often are. Therefore, instead of assuming and looking like a know-it-all or making an error in judgment, try to find out all that you can. Ask the person how you can help. Propose solutions to problems the person perceives with your idea.

If you at least show that you are trying to see something from someone else's perspective, then you make a good impression. You prove that you care about others besides yourself and you possess the priceless quality of empathy. Even if you don't entirely get it, say that you understand and honestly attempt to understand.

Be Sympathetic With The Other Person's Ideas And Desires

Sympathy is the unique ability to see what a person is

feeling and respond to it appropriately, without pushing your own agenda on the other person. If someone feels strongly about something, it is in your best interest to recognize that and address his or her feelings.

Often, people tend to get defensive when someone criticizes their ideas. You can stand out from the crowd by being sympathetic instead. When someone points out an issue with your idea, you can sympathize with how they feel and try to find a way to work with them toward a solution.

Saying "I understand how you feel" can make a world of difference when speaking with someone. You appear much more well-rounded and empathetic when you attempt to understand them. The person will automatically feel more of a connection with you and even a sense of loyalty based on reciprocity [4].

Dramatize Your Ideas

Carnegie was a big fan of "dramatizing your ideas." He felt this was the best way to get people to listen to your ideas and possibly share them. But what did he mean by this?

Drama captures people's attention. You have probably been to presentations or speeches where the person bored you to sleep. Death by PowerPoint, where someone uses boring slides to drive home a point, is one example of an idea being presented in a boring way. Yet you have probably also been to presentations where you were riveted. Your attention was totally captivated by this person's ability to convey his or her idea and you didn't stop paying attention through the end. A good TedTalk can have this effect. Think about both experiences; what was the difference between the two?

Dramatizing your ideas involves presenting them in a way that makes people pay attention. It grabs them somewhere internally and gives them a good reason to keep listening. It is more than some fancy fonts and bright colors in a presentation – it involves speaking in a way that appeals to the listener.

Pathos, ethos, and logos are three good elements to any presentation. You use these three things to get someone to identify with your idea either emotionally, ethically, or logically. They are the fundamental elements of any good speech for this reason, but they are also crucial for any idea presentation of any form. Pathos entails the emotional aspect of something. How will it make the listener feel? ASPCA commercials with videos of sad dogs are designed to appeal to pathos. You might think about adding drama to your idea by showing the listener how someone is suffering, or how a group is impacted negatively. You might also think about how someone may be personally affected by an idea and use that to appeal to him or her. Both techniques are equally effective, but you can find one or the other more effective for an individual situation.

For instance, if you are trying to convince someone to support your endeavor for a new hurricane response strategy, you could start by talking about how families of Hurricane Katrina are still struggling even fourteen years later. But for a personal impact, you could talk about the person's relatives who were impacted by a hurricane. If the person lives in a coastal area, you could even appeal to his fear by talking about what could happen to his home and his family should your strategy not be put in place.

Ethos involves ethics. Most people have strong ethics and a clear sense of right and wrong. They will do what they think is right or stand up for you if you are doing what they think is right. Showing someone how your idea solves an ethical dilemma can get a person on board. Proposing a new way to help victims of sex trafficking might involve appealing to everyone's ethics about human slavery. Listing things wrong with a current law and how it ethically harms people is a good way to get people to vote to repeal the law.

You can even play on people's sense of righteousness and show them how they are being wronged if they don't act in support of your idea.

Logos is simply logic. Some people don't want to hear about emotion – they don't care or it's not applicable in a certain situation. Your boss or a potential investor may be such a person. They don't want to hear how your idea will make them feel, they want to hear about how your idea will logically fit into their work and make things at the company better. You want to use lots of logos when you are making a business proposition, for instance.

Now, a blend of all three works quite well. You want to appeal to someone's ethics and emotions at once. Then you want to appeal to their logic by talking about the logistics of your idea, or how it will work and what it will entail.

The truth is always a good place to start. But simply

stating the truth in a monotonous tone is not going to win you any followers. Rather, you must portray the truth in a way that shocks, triggers, and engages people. In other words, you must use the above-mentioned concepts and some dramatic effect to make the truth seem a bit more dramatic.

Compare the speaker who just stands there delivering dry words to the one who waves his arms, moves around the podium, and gets the audience to repeat after him. Getting people involved in your speech by engaging with them and using vivid language and large body language is a surefire way to arouse excitement and passion in others.

If you must use pictures or a PowerPoint, deviate from the norm. Don't just show some graphs and call it a day. Use pictures that will shock and horrify people, or pictures that will make people happy. Use bright colors and big fonts to make your ideas more tangible. Interesting presentations involve shapes, colors, and fonts that are unusual, but still clearly legible.

In fact, people tend to have more of a neural response to visually stimulating images or presentations [12]. There is a caveat, however. A convoluted image or graph showing tons of information will be too complex for the brain to grasp, so it will give up and the person will lose interest. A simple image that can be understood in a glance is far more effective. You will have more luck selling a new cleaning product by showing a stained shirt transforming into a clean one than by showing a bunch of pictures or some convoluted plot graph that indicates cleanliness. You will get more people to donate to your homelessness prevention cause if you show a picture or video of a homeless person with frostbite than a weird graphic showing how homeless people are victims of cold weather.

In Carnegie's book *How to Win Friends and*

Influence People, he shared a story about a company who used live rats in their window display for selling rat poison [5]. Their sales increased by five times. Doing something wild and creative that stands out in someone's mind is the way to drive people to respond to your ideas. An illustration, picture, or something even wilder like live rats can make your idea seem more real and more memorable.

In fact, using something tangible is a great way to dramatize an idea. The live rats are a great example of how you can use a real item or object to sell a product. To be a salesman of your product or idea, you must make it real and concrete. You must use showmanship to target your listener and turn him into a lead.

Don't waste your time on dry facts, boring statistics, or long-winded speeches. No one has the patience. Most people will give you eight seconds to get their attention, and then ten to twenty minutes once you have it [13]. If you don't capture their attention in that eight-second window, you have lost it for good and you won't get those ten to twenty minutes to make your point. Open your presentation with something really impactful or tangible and then you are free to offer a condensed version of the dull logistics for a longer time after your bold opening.

Getting to know your target is a great way to figure out the dramatizing aspect. Find out everything you can about the person you are pitching your idea to. Learn their preferences, the things that emotionally aggravate them, their ethical stance on certain things, and their commitments. Then find a way to bend your idea to appeal to something you learned about that person. If you can't do research on the person you are pitching to, then you can ask the person yourself, "How do you feel about [insert idea here]?" Judging by their response, you can formulate something dramatic that will catch their attention.

Many people fit into a demographic that makes it easier to appeal to them as a whole. Commercials use this relentlessly, targeting housewives for cleaning products and young frat boys for fast food. If your idea is targeted to a certain demographic, look into advertising targeting that demographic and tailor your presentation to be like those ads. Treating your idea presentation like an advertisement, short, sweet, and appealing, is an ideal way to hook people.

Chapter 4: Improving Your Conversations

Obviously, you want to improve your conversations or you wouldn't be reading this book. There are several means by which you can do this. The following sections offer various ways to be more interesting, more fun, and more positive so that people will like you more. The result to using these techniques is that you will see more returns from your conversations, such as business leads, friends, repeat clients, or dates.

How To Be More Likable

The big question everyone has is how to be more likable. Being more likable is not always easy, nor is it a simple recipe that you can follow. You just have to change your behavior a bit and be able to engage in conversations well in order to be more likable.

Not everyone is going to like you. Accepting this truth

is part of what will make you more likable. As you become comfortable with the fact that you are who you are and not everyone has to like you in order for you to feel validated, you reach a new level of confidence and comfort that infuses confidence and comfort in those around you.

There is no magic formula that will make people like you, either. Since each person is different, your interactions will be different as well. You can raise your chances of having someone like you by embracing those differences and tailoring your conversations to fit each new person you meet. This means that you need to be accepting and even curious about differences, you need to ask lots of questions to get to know someone, and you need to listen and provide the best responses. You also need to read social cues and be sensitive to shifts in the conversation, such as when a person feels uncomfortable or annoyed with what you are saying.

For example, if you are meeting someone who is a vegan, saying things like, "How can you not like meat!? Meat is delicious! I just love a juicy steak, right off the grill. Yum!" is not helpful. Instead, you might try to find out why this person has chosen a vegan diet. You might also try to mention that you are a carnivore but you respect veganism and you like certain vegan recipes that you have tried. By doing this, you show that you try to find things in common rather than pointing out differences, and you also show curiosity and respect for the differences that do arise. This instantly makes you more likable.

Being sensitive to cultural differences and attempting to understand how to approach people of different cultures is a huge plus, as it denotes your willingness to accommodate others and respect their unique beliefs. It is impossible to learn the nuances of every single culture on the face of the Earth, but if you try to learn about cultures and if you ask someone directly about their cultural values, you show an eagerness to accommodate them that they will appreciate.

Being funny is another big one [14]. Most women say that humor is important in the man they want to meet, for instance [14]. If you are naturally humorous, let that shine through. Make jokes and make the other person laugh to increase affection. If you are not humorous, that's OK too. Avoid forcing jokes, as that will just become awkward. Be comfortable with the fact that you are not a jokester. People will respect you more for accepting who you are than trying to be someone whom you are not.

How To Be More Friendly And Social

A friendly and social person has the extroverted characteristics of talking to people, including strangers, like old friends. He or she sets people at ease by talking first and dominating the conversation. He or she smiles a lot and is happy to give hugs.

Observe these characteristics and then adopt them into your social interactions. You can appear friendly, even if you are a shy person, simply by changing how you approach others.

First, you want to convey warmth by smiling a lot and being very open to people. This requires open body language. Open body language entails facing a person with your whole body, not just your face. Turning away even slightly can create a subconscious blockage, which can terminate the conversation quickly [15]. Face the person, lean toward them, and have your legs and arms uncrossed. Don't point your feet toward an exit or away from the person, as this shows that you are dying to get away from the conversation [15]. Make eye contact and lots of it. Touch the person now and then, such as lightly on the arm, to create a sort of subconscious connection [15].

Talk first. Be the first to go up to someone and smile and say hi. Introduce yourself and find out everything you can about the person. Pay attention to what they say so that you can bring up those details later. People value it when you remember things about them, such as their name, birthday, and other details.

Engage the person by asking them lots of questions. Then actually listen to their responses. Don't just wait for your turn to talk. Show you're listening by nodding empathetically, saying "yes" often, and even asking more relevant questions or asking the person to elaborate on something he or she said.

You should also be open about yourself. You want to tell the person who you are and give quite a few details so that they feel as if they are getting to know you. You don't want to just monopolize the conversation talking about yourself, but rather seek a balance between volunteering information about yourself and asking them information about themselves. Talking and listening go hand in hand when being friendly. You must do both equally well.

If you watch a friendly person, you will notice that his body language and gestures are usually big and broad, and upbeat. He is always smiling, waving his hands around, and holding his head up high. Seeming happy can make others feel happy, almost like a mirror response [16]. Happiness is pretty contagious [16]. So much so, that people who are around someone who expresses happiness have a 25% higher chance of being happy themselves [16]. Just as people are interrelated, so are their emotions, as people tend to mimic the emotions they see in the other person. So, your job as a friendly person is to lead the way by being happy. Appearing happy will make people feel good so they enjoy your company more. Being miserable will drive people away, on the other hand.

The final main part of friendliness involves a willingness to keep a connection in the future. You don't just have a conversation for the sake of having one. You invite the person to meet you for coffee later and leave your number, or you invite the person to join you at an event you think he or she may enjoy. Using thoughtfulness, you find what a person may like to do and ensure that you do it together.

When you see someone you have spoken to before, you say hi and you remember who that person is. A willingness to greet and remember details about people is a sign that you are invested in the relationship. It also opens communication again and again. The warm fuzzy feeling it gives the other person is cause for future talks, as well, since you just offered that person a form of praise by engaging him or her again.

Nevertheless, you don't just talk to people you know. You talk to people you don't know. You are always happy to meet new people and extend your friends group farther. Friendly people are outgoing because they like people and show a genuine interest in them. They want to make friends, hence the term "friendly." Therefore, your behavior must reflect your inherent desire to make friends and do things outside of yourself. Think of how that would look and try it out.

How To Be More Fun

What makes a person fun? The most common elements of a fun person are a sense of humor, confidence, and a willingness to be daring and bold in trying new things. Moreover, a fun person is not a negative person, meaning he doesn't complain, condemn, criticize, or even gossip.

Fun people generally smile a lot, and their smiles are genuine. The more you smile, the more you make others happy [16]. Your ability to be fun involves making others feel good and free.

You also don't make people feel inhibited. Being judgmental, closeted, or reserved can make others feel uncomfortable and unwilling to be themselves. You must be open and talk about crazy things. When people talk about crazy things as well, you listen and laugh rather than acting mortified or shocked.

The fun person may be the one who suggests spin the bottle at a party. Or the one who jumps off the boat at a yacht party. The fun person is always looking for wild new things for everyone to do. If an idea pops into your head, don't be shy about suggesting it. You may seem crazy or even get shot down, but you appear less inhibited, which causes others to follow suit.

You also say yes more. A fun person is not going to hang back out of shyness while everyone else plays a game. The fun person jumps into the game, eager to win. You want to challenge people to games, invite them to do fun things after the event, or at least agree to do what they suggest. You don't turn down invitations, but rather go along, curious to see what each new opportunity may bring.

Enthusiasm is the hallmark of a fun person. Think of a fun teacher or coach you had. The difference between this role model and other teachers or coaches was probably the warmth, passion, and enthusiasm this person showed you. You felt eager to do what he wanted because he instilled a sense of wonder and spread enthusiasm through the room. Therefore, be enthusiastic as you talk to people. Express lots of interest. Express enthusiasm when you receive invitations and say yes emphatically.

Don't let your fears or shyness inhibit you. You must have confidence that makes you bold. For instance, if you are shy about how you look in a swimsuit, you could turn down an invitation to a really fun pool party. Then you just missed out on a great memory and some great possible friendships. Instead, find a flattering swimsuit and stop worrying about your body, focusing instead on having fun and enjoying yourself. If you don't let fear get in the way, you are more open to having fun and trying new things, which makes you a fun person.

Furthermore, you don't just darken the mood with complaining, which drives others to complain. You lighten the mood by finding the silver lining to every situation that you would otherwise complain about. As your positivity becomes contagious, people like you more because you are upbeat and you make them look at life in a more fun way.

How To Be More Interesting

Interesting people have not always led interesting lives. You may meet an insurance salesman from a small town who has a very ordinary life, yet he still proves to be interesting. The key to being interesting is giving others interesting conversations, not having some long list of overwhelming stories about encounters with crocodiles and getting away with larceny and spending your summer in Europe.

If you have led an interesting life, then you can

certainly share that. Your interesting stories can entertain others. The caveat is that many people feel that their lives are interesting and their stories are entertaining – when they are anything but. You may tell some stories but gauge the reactions of others. Are they listening because they are hooked, or because they feel obligated? You can tell by whether or not they make eye contact and whether or not their facial expressions follow the appropriate moods of your story. Laughter, leaning in toward you, and nodding a lot are also affirmations that someone likes your story.

Beyond this, you should not just make stories all about you. You should focus on making them about those around you. Draw stories out of people by asking things like, "So you seem like an interesting person. Why don't you tell me about yourself?"

People are most interested in conversations where they can speak about themselves. No one enjoys any subject as much as one that involves him. So, encouraging others to speak and share things about themselves is key to an interesting conversation.

First, you may want to start the conversation by bringing up something interesting about yourself. Tell a story or mention something that happened earlier in the day. Give others time to respond and then let them come up with their similar stories. People will be glad to share stories that may be only minimally related, or not related at all, to what you said. At least you have given them the fodder to form conversation with, and you have broken the ice. Now they will happily take over the conversation.

A truly interesting, stimulating conversation involves some give and take. First, you speak, then someone else speaks, then you respond. These conversations often only thrive when you are speaking about a subject you are both familiar with and interested in.

Academic, professional, and hobby-centered conversations can achieve this. But so can regular conversations between two people who have found something in common. Spend some time sharing things about yourself and asking questions to find that sweet spot, that topic you can both elaborate on.

The conversation may even involve many topics. Be flexible and willing to switch between topics without resistance. You can always bring up a subject you really want to talk about and see where the conversation goes from there. Conversations are seldom predictable, which is what makes them even more interesting. Therefore, be open to a lack of predictability.

Storytelling In Social Situations

If you have a great story to share, by all means, share it. But when telling stories in conversation, you must adhere to some rules.

The first rule is to determine if the subject of your story is suited to this conversation. If you are having dinner with your new partner's parents and you start telling raunchy stories about your latest sexual escapades, well, you may just blow the whole impression you are trying to make. Usually, it is pretty obvious if your story is suitable. Think about the audience and how your story may appeal to them or offend them.

The next rule is to make sure your story is short and sweet. A long-winded story with tons of details and side stories may be entertaining at heart and even have a satisfying conclusion or point, but you lose your listeners in the maze of unnecessary details. Cut out the unnecessary details. No one needs to know what you ordered for dinner on your trip to Niagara Falls, unless, of course, the story centers around how good the food was or something hilarious that happened relating to the food. Find the irrelevant details and skip over them so that your story is no longer than five minutes. Try to keep the story linear and on a reasonable timeline so that listeners are not lost in a maze of side stories.

The third rule involves reading social cues as you talk. You may think your story is the most fascinating one ever told, but others will quickly show you if this is not the case. Be sure to wrap up your story more quickly if people start shifting and looking at exits or the clock. Talk more if people seem enthralled. If people look angry, you may just want to smooth over the offense you have caused.

Finally, be sure that your story has emotional relevance, or at least relevance to the conversation at hand. If you must tell a random story, say, "I'm sorry, I just had to share this thing that happened to me. It's unrelated but I think you'll appreciate it." Your story must make people feel bad, laugh, tense up in suspense, or even recoil in disgust. An emotional response makes listeners feel more invested in the story and more intrigued by how it is resolved.

A good story must also have a riveting beginning to catch the listener's interest, an entertaining middle without too many cluttered details, and a satisfying resolution. You may even give your story a mysterious ending – "No one knows who did it to this day!" Either way, the story has obviously and officially ended and it is memorable for what it entailed.

People only like to listen to what you say about yourself if they have a buy-in. The buy-in would be an emotional response or a point to relate on. They will only listen if they think that they can respond. You will lose their attention very rapidly if you don't give them a reason to listen.

When Having A Quiet Voice Hampers Your Social Success

Would you believe that the volume and sound of your

voice has a huge impact on how much other people listen to you, respect you, and even like you? A quiet voice can make you seem like a mouse and no one is inclined to pay you any mind. You should work on increasing the volume of your voice to command attention.

You have noticed loud people in the past. This is because their loud voices demand that everyone listens to them. The volume forces you to pay attention. A quiet voice does not have this effect.

In fact, women are at a disadvantage for this reason. Most people find deep, loud voices the most attractive when it comes to conversation [17]. In fact, in a study where people were given recordings of voices and asked to rate what they assumed the person behind the voice looked like, they rated the men with "attractive voices" as being the most attractive [17]. Other research shows that those with attractive voices tend to have more sexual partners and engage in infidelity more often [18]. And women who are speaking to men they find more attractive tend to use higher-pitched voices, which in turn men find more attractive [19]. This research indicates that your voice plays a huge role in how others perceive you and how your social interaction goes. It can possibly be the difference between a second date or never hearing from your date again.

The simple truth is that being quiet means you won't get noticed as much. So, you may speak, but you notice that people look away or talk over you. They simply are not paying attention to your words because your voice is not commanding them to pay attention and your words are not registering in their brain. You must stand out by speaking up. Practice at home if you have a quiet voice and get confident raising your voice in social situations.

Reasons Someone May See You As Weird

Have you ever been accused of being weird? Perhaps

it wasn't a compliment, but rather an insult. You can't figure out why you are weird. You see some of your oddities, but everyone has them. Some people who are openly weird are embraced in social situations, while others are ostracized. Why does your particular brand of weirdness get you ostracized?

There are several factors that make you seem weird. The first is that you have ideas that clash with the ideas others have, which is certainly not always a bad thing. But if you are bringing up conspiracy theories that have no rational basis, or talking about how your neighbors watch you, you make others question your sanity. Your ideas are simply too incongruent with what is socially acceptable.

Another reason might be that you refuse to take responsibility for life. You may feel that life is beyond your control. With this mindset, you let a lot of things "happen" to you and then complain about your lack of luck. People find this aggravating and immature.

They want to see you make some effort to get the outcomes you want. Not taking accountability is a habit that makes people lose response for you.

Another habit is feeling that happiness is unobtainable. Your depressing conversation drives others away as you go on and on about how hopeless everything is. Your eternal dark mood will infect others, making them want to avoid you because you are simply too sad to be around. The fact that emotions are contagious is why this happens [16]. This behavior may seem cute when you are fifteen, but it is no longer desirable when you reach adulthood.

Thinking that you are a rock star when in fact you are a computer geek is another form of weirdness that can drive people away. People love seeing confidence, but they often draw the line at pure narcissism. If you think that you are somehow extraordinary and you try to prove it all of the time, or you must brag and one-up everyone around you, then conversation with you becomes a competition. Most people won't bother taking the bait and find that talking to you is exhausting.

Yet another form of weirdness is comparing yourself to others and letting your insecurities shine through in your conversations. You are a unique person and you should own that fact. Not doing so makes you seem both miserable and full of doubt. You may also appear envious, as you talk about how others have things much better than you do. You engage in more complaining when you are in this mindset, too. People prefer confidence, so they see this as a deterrent.

Finally, holding some sort of weird opinion about yourself to excuse your behavior is a weird factor that people find unattractive. If you say that you can't work in a certain environment because you have the wrong personality type, or you don't "do" negativity because you are a highly sensitive person, or you are chronically late because you have a certain Circadian rhythm, you are basically explaining your behavior with flawed (and often baseless) research. You are making up excuses as opposed to simply owning your personality. Stop making excuses and simply apologize that a certain job isn't right for you, you're not in the mood to hear complaining tonight, or you are very sorry that you are late.

Social Mistakes Intellectual People Make

Intellectual people have an advantage: they can't stand small talk, mainly because they don't see the point to it. This is great because small talk is detrimental to conversations. Good conversations have some depth and are far more interesting than simply exchanging notes on the weather or last night's Cowboys game.

But intellectual people can also have a disadvantage. They tend to engage in certain mistakes that create conversational barriers. They impede further social interaction with these habits. You don't have to engage in these habits, no matter how smart you really are. A truly smart person understands that social interaction is just as important as AIDS research, and thus he tries to improve his life by building solid social foundations.

The first habit is underestimating the intelligence of everyone else in the room. You adopt an attitude that you are somehow superior. You tell people, "I would explain that but you wouldn't understand it. It's very complex." This kills the conversation immediately because you are basically insulting everyone around you with your superior attitude.

Another mistake is overestimating others' interest in dull facts. You bore people with death by statistics, citing complicated research studies and numbers that no one cares about. Your conversation lacks substance as you attempt to prove how smart you are.

Always remember to dramatize your ideas by making them intriguing to others [5].

Intellectual people also tend to assume that they are always right. They block communication by refusing to hear others' ideas and by showing no interest in what others have to say. They argue themselves blue in the face. Remember that the best argument tactic is not engaging in an argument at all [5]. There is no need to prove that you are right. Simply make your point and then invite discourse. If people disagree with you, you can politely try to win them over to your ideas, but you can't make anyone agree with you.

A final big mistake is monopolizing the conversation. You may think that your philosophical diatribe or your academic research is the most fascinating thing in the world – and you can make it seem so by giving lively discussion about it. But if you go on and on, especially to a person who is clearly bored, then you are being selfish. You are not letting the other person speak or share ideas. You are simply holding the soapbox until everyone is done with the conversation, yet you are still talking. Be sure to let others speak and offer opinions. Ask others questions as well.

Being Too Negative In Social Situations

Negative Nancy and Debbie Downer are both real people. You have probably met them. Their capacity for souring any conversation and ruining any party with constant complaining, comparing, and sharing inappropriately sad things are unrivaled. Don't be like them.

A lot of negative people do this because it is a habit [2]. Being negative for a long period of time is what rewires their brains to always dwell on negative things. Rewiring your brain by talking about positive things for once can help you make more people feel good, leading to better conversations.

They may also simply not know any better. Their negativity is a way they use to communicate. They think that complaining helps them commiserate with others because they don't know better ways to bond with others. They think that sharing sad stories is the only way to get people to relate to them and give them attention. They think gossiping is the only way to get friends, as they bond with others over a mutual dislike of someone. Realize that none of these habits lead to solid bonds based on affection. You will simply drive people away. Work instead on forming bonds by talking about things you both love and giving compliments.

These people also tend to believe that negativity and pessimism are signs of intellectualism, when in fact they are signs of having nothing better to talk about. You do not appear brilliant because you depress everyone as you lecture parties about ocean acidification; you only seem brilliant when you discuss your ideas for how to reverse that problem.

Showing solutions instead of making complaints shows people a more intellectual and thoughtful side of you.

Some people have been through a lot and it becomes habit to complain about their situations. But you must realize that complaining is basically making others deal with your problems. It also proves that you don't have the ability to solve issues in your life. Avoid complaining about the horrible things that have happened to you, even if you have been through a lot. No one owes you anything, not even sympathy. Complaining will simply sour the conversation so shift it to lighter subjects. Don't make your conversation partners be the victims of your emotions and bad situations that are out of their control. Save that for your therapist.

Sarcasm is the lowest form of wit. It is also a common form of negativity that people express in an attempt to be funny and to protect themselves from real emotions. Trading sarcasm for a more enlightened form of humor can help you make more real social bonds.

Some people just have negative personality traits that they over-express. A tendency to be judgmental, or to complain a lot, or to compare things that are not related are all personality traits that become habit. But you would be wise to change these traits, or at least downplay them. Express a negative trait in the occasional dark joke or complaint but keep the majority of your conversation light and positive to make others like talking to you more.

You may also be depressed, which causes you to have a negative view of the world as a symptom. Seek treatment right away. Unchecked depression is bound to get worse.

You may think that by lowering your standards, you are improving the odds that you will be impressed, which seldom works. Try to look at the positive and let that impress you more. Showing positivity is always more appreciated than darkening everyone's day with your need to keep your standards low.

Being Too Secretive And Guarded

Have you ever spoken with someone who would not disclose anything about him- or herself? The conversation can get very uncomfortable as you feel forced to fill the void with more details about yourself. You also leave feeling as if you don't know the person you were talking to.

If you make this same mistake, you can make people walk away feeling as if you are a stranger still. Since the point of a conversation is to get to know someone and determine if you would like to have future conversations, you would be wise to avoid being too secretive and guarded. Otherwise, you leave a lot of questions and a sense of discomfort with the other person.

Conversations require a fine balance between sharing too little and sharing too much. Both are bad habits. You want to share just enough to give the other person a sense of who you are, without going into too much detail and sharing your whole life story and personal things that are best left for therapists or very dear friends.

When you are too secretive and guarded, you remove the other person's ability to determine if he or she likes you. You rob the conversation of its ability to open a relationship. This is a communication barrier that the other person can't be expected to overcome on his or her own.

Therefore, you must divulge some things about yourself. When a person brings up a topic, mention how it relates to you. When a person says he has three dogs, mention your pet. Try to mention things that are relevant to the conversation and share stories to illuminate the other person as to who you are.

Some people communicate by focusing on the other person, while others communicate by focusing on themselves. Both types can be annoying and can stop conversation by taking the bonding experience away from the equation. You can stop this by sharing some things, asking questions about the other person, and commenting on what the other person says. Be open and also listen well. A good conversation possesses elements of both behaviors.

Chapter 5: Listening Skills

So far you have learned how to speak and act in conversations. But the most important element of any conversation is listening. If you listen, you understand the other person and you show it. You express interest which is a form of praise. Only then can the conversation develop into something more.

Having polished listening skills seems easy, except few people are truly good listeners. You can learn how to listen well and improve conversations thusly. Then you stand out from the crowd with superior listening abilities that few possess.

Why You Should Listen More Than You Talk

The first big reason why you should listen more than you talk involves being present and mindful of the conversation. If you are listening, then you are in a prime place to receive information. You get the complete picture of what the person is saying. Only then can you come up with a wholesome, effective solution to the problem at hand or a response that works for what the other person has said. With this response, you drive the conversation forward, and make the person feel placated or heard.

Think about when your boss is chewing you out for doing something wrong. You could tune your boss out because you hate being criticized, and then keep making the mistake and getting in trouble. Or you could really listen and figure out how to avoid future trouble.

Listening also helps you get to know the person you are talking to, so that you can think of responses that work in context. You get what the person is saying and you are able to keep the conversation going. You show that you are invested, which can make the person want to keep talking. If someone is telling you how she feels, for instance, you would show that you understood by saying, "I understand why you would feel that way." Then you have some valuable information about who that person is and what that person feels. You can use that information to avoid making the person feel that way in the future.

Finally, listening helps you give the other praise by showing interest in what they are saying. People can tell when you are not listening. You look bored, or you come up with irrelevant responses, or you are paying more attention to things other than the person who is speaking. The person feels understood and validated when you hone in and prove that you are listening by leaning in to the other person, making eye contact, nodding at appropriate times, and coming up with responses directly related to what he or she is saying.

Listening Is More Than Merely Hearing

You can hear what someone says. But listening involves actually processing and using the information you gained from listening. It is a step farther than hearing: It is hearing someone's words and then using them to construct meaning that makes sense. It is using that meaning to come up with what you say next. It is also using that meaning to determine how to approach and work with the person in the future.

You will obviously hear something a person says to you because their voice creates sound waves that reach your ears. But you *choose* to listen. Making that choice can validate the other person. There is nothing more frustrating than a conversation where the person receives what you said with a blank face and then responses with something totally off-subject. If you do the opposite and actually listen, then you make a good impression.

How To Effectively Listen

The first part of listening involves body language. You must express you are listening with physical gestures. The first and more important is leaning into the person, looking at them, and keeping your body oriented toward them [15]. Eye contact is also important here. It shows a total focus on the person in front of you, which encourages him or her to keep talking.

The second part is minimizing distractions or ignoring them. Don't keep checking your phone, gazing off into space, or watching the TV rather than the person. By tuning out distractions, you give your sole focus to the person you are talking to. Many people find that they can listen while they multitask. This may be true, but science suggests that multitasking is not really possible [20]. Besides, even if you can multitask, most people take that as a sign that you are not really listening at all. If you must check your phone, say, "I'm sorry, but I really have to get this. I am listening and I want to hear more."

The third part is not thinking about what you are going to say next. A lot of people listen only to think of how to respond. They are busy thinking of advice that no one has asked for or an opinion. If you clear your head to think only about what the other person is saying, you can give real responses as they naturally occur. For instance, if someone is talking about their cat dying, you think about this and it makes you sad. That comes across on your face. Then you prove that you are listening and absorbing what they say.

There are several different kinds of listening. They are all effective depending on the situation. Learning about them helps you pick the kind that is more effective for your situation to yield the best results.

Different Kinds of Listening

Discriminative listening is the kind of listening babies first develop. They can't respond back, but they can differentiate between sounds and thus derive meaning [21]. It is the least effective because it only gives you basic meaning, without any emotional or informational details. You may use this when you are listening for someone to say your name or you are trying to get the gist of a conversation you just walked in on.

Pseudo-listening is where you are pretending to listen when you are really daydreaming. You say "Uh-huh" at appropriate moments and pay attention to something else. People tend to use this when they really don't care about what someone is saying [21]. It is not effective for conversation at all.

Appreciative listening is when you listen without really delving into the substance of the conversation [21]. This is what you do when listening to your favorite song or watching a movie in a language you don't understand just because you like how the words sound. It is also not effective because you are just appreciating the sounds, not the actual content.

Informational listening, or comprehensive listening,

is like when you pay attention to a lecture or an informational broadcast to get information. You are listening to learn [21]. Do this when you are trying to learn something or gather what is being expressed.

The problem with this kind of listening is that you are merely taking in information. You are not keeping an emotional balance in the other person or feeding conversation. Informational listening is best for one-sided conversations or lectures, not personal conversations.

Next, you have critical listening [21]. Just like its name, this is when you are reviewing the information you receive simply to give a response. You may use this when you are listening to a politician giving a speech or someone asking your opinion. You hear simply to figure out how you feel and how you want to respond.

Most people use this level of listening in all

conversations, which keeps them from getting the full meaning of deep conversations. They are attempting to think of what they will say and how they feel instead of focusing on the speaker.

Sympathetic listening is slightly better. It is where you listen and then respond in sympathy [21]. You understand the person and you express that with a sympathetic nod or saying "Yes" sometimes. You may even wait for your turn to speak and offer some great advice. You are showing listening and caring, which is great. But this listening is still missing something: the ability to see through someone's words, grasp the full meaning of what they say, and attempt to help them. Providing sympathetic listening is not bad, but you can improve that even more with empathetic listening.

Empathetic listening is the final and most advanced form of listening, which is useful in personal conversations [21]. This is where you fully attempt to understand what the other person is saying or feeling. You are listening in order to maintain a relationship and possibly help the other person. Empathetic listening calls for empathy, where you attempt to feel what the other person is feeling and you attempt to give a good response that the person can appreciate. You listen more than you talk and you give valid responses that relate only to what the other person is saying, not what you want to say. You refrain from giving opinions and advice, and simply listen instead. This conversation is not about you, it's about the other person. You express this with your body language and reflective listening.

Empathetic listening is useful in all situations. You can use it with your boss, to show that you understand how he feels and how you plan to make it better. You can use it as your spouse talks about a long, boring day at the office to make him or her feel better. You can use it as your friend describes a break-up to let him or her vent and process emotions. You can even use it on strangers, making yourself seem like the best listener and most empathetic person in the universe. This listening makes you a better friend and a stronger partner, which is why it is so important. Plus, it is rare, so you will stand out from the crowd this way.

Reflective Listening

Reflective listening is a skill that adds to your empathetic listening and helps you gain a complete understanding of the other person. The idea is that you use gestures and facial expressions to reflect back what someone is saying.

This is not just a skill that self-help books push on people; it is widely used in therapy and corporate training [22]. In an evaluation of people who used reflective listening in their first interactions, the conversation partners were quick to rate more satisfaction with the conversations that used reflective listening and lower satisfaction with the conversations that contained simple acknowledgments, or sympathetic listening [22]. The basic point is that you can enrich your conversations with reflective listening.

Reflective Responses Provide A Mirror To The Speaker

Reflective listening is a form of empathetic listening that reflects back what the other person has said. You create a mirror for their words, helping them see that you are listening while also helping them process whatever they are trying to unburden on you. By doing this, you make someone hear themselves talk while also gaining a more comprehensive understanding yourself. You can make sure that you heard things correctly and understand things fully. Thus, reflective listening benefits both parties in a conversation.

Reflective listening is very active. It involves listening well, processing information at a rapid rate, and coming up with responses that basically repeat or paraphrase what someone has said. It also may call for you to give agreement, disagreement, or advice, but you should wait to see if someone asks. A lot of people don't want your advice or opinion, they simply want to vent.

Always use reflective listening in conversations, particularly with new people. Prove your investment by taking the time to understand the full conversation and reiterate it back. Let people process their emotions in personal talks by reflecting back what they are saying, giving them a more abstract glimpse of what they are really trying to communicate. Also, use it if you don't understand something in order to let the person give you a better understanding.

Furthermore, you can avoid miscommunication this way by ensuring that you get the message correctly and letting the person correct any mistakes in communication. You avoid making the wrong decision based on misunderstood information.

Plus, you can avoid being bored or distracted because reflective listening calls for a lot of focus. You must take an active part in the conversation. You can't daydream and fail to pay attention while using reflective listening; the very act forces you to listen to everything the other person says.

Paraphrasing

To reflect what someone has said, you can paraphrase what they have said in a few words or sentences that capture the gist of the conversation. You thus show that you understand what was said and the main points being made. Paraphrasing does not mean that you must repeat everything someone said, as that will certainly be redundant and boring. Instead, you sum it up. You show that you have understood and retained the main relevant bits.

Paraphrasing can help make sure you heard everything correctly. The other person can then correct you if you misunderstood something. You can also lead the conversation into a mutual discussion by paraphrasing and inviting further discourse on the topic.

Reflecting Feelings

"So, you must feel angry that he cut you off?" This is an example of how to reflect someone's feelings. You infer what someone is feeling and express it in a way that they can agree with or disagree with. It invites further discussion about the person's feelings.

Some people express what they are feeling clearly. In that case, you can say, "I understand why you feel that way." These conversations make reflective listening easy.

But a lot of people don't say their feelings outright. They imply them. That is why you must ask, "So you feel this way?" You give the person a chance to either agree or disagree, so that you gain a more complete picture of the person's emotional response. For instance, if someone is talking about a break-up, you could say, "So you feel very lonely now?" The person may say yes, or he may say, "No, I'm just mad!"

When you reflect someone's feelings, you are validating their feelings. You are suggesting that their feelings are normal. You also prove that you care about their emotions. Furthermore, you can learn a lot about how someone reacts to events and situations. If a person is mad that someone is late, you can gather that being late is that person's pet peeve and you can avoid being late in the future to stay on the person's good side. This is especially useful in ongoing relationships, allowing you to really get to know a person at a depth that most people lack.

Reflecting Meanings

An example of reflecting someone's meaning would be, "So you mean that you are quitting?" You are paraphrasing, asking for clarification, and proving that you are listening, all in one. You want to do this often to make sure you understand just what is being said. The other person will appreciate your effort to understand everything.

Often, people fail to be clear about what they mean. They use metaphors and analogies, they hint at their meanings, or they skate around their points. You have to be discerning and ask what the person means. Simply asking, "What is your point?" sounds terse and rude. But asking, "I am trying to understand what you mean. Could you clarify things for me?" is far more effective. Sometimes you may even have to guess and ask if your guess is correct.

Once a person clarifies something, you can avoid operating on assumptions, which is always dangerous. Imagine a scenario where your romantic partner is angry about your behavior but does not specifically tell you what behavior triggered that anger. If you assume what the person is mad about, then you may go about correcting the wrong behavior and keep performing the one that is so enraging to your partner. But if you ask and find out just what your partner is mad about, you can pinpoint what exactly you must change. You also make the relationship stronger, as you attempt to listen to and validate the other person's feelings and improve yourself for the relationship to run smoothly.

Why Words Mean Little

Words mean little. Why? Because people often don't say what they really mean, or they lie. A person may say she is fine when she is clearly not, for instance.

Communication goes much deeper than the spoken word. With most of human communication being unspoken, you can assume that words are pretty meaningless [23]. Only seven percent of human language is thought to be verbal, anyway.

It is far more important to pay attention to the other ninety-three percent: body language, facial expression, movements, and tone [23]. These things give you better clues about what someone really means. Back to the example about the girl who says she is fine, you can tell that she is really not fine by her tears. Then you can ask her what is wrong and find out the real problem, instead of taking her word for it and dropping the whole thing, as a bad friend would do.

Listen With Your Eyes, Not Just Your Ears

A conversation is so much more than the words spoken. By observing how someone looks, moves, and acts, you can gather a range of information. Listening with your eyes involves paying attention to facial expressions and body language. It gives you a wealth of information that lets you see through the words someone is saying to get the bigger picture.

For example, if someone tells you that she is excited

about a new job opportunity but she looks nervous, you can tell a lot about how she is really feeling. Then you can make her feel heard and able to talk to you more by saying, "You seem nervous. What do you really feel about this opportunity?" Imagine how great she will feel that you understand her so well and care about how she really feels. You just showed genuine interest!

Another cool feature of this skill is seeing through someone's lies. You can see when their feelings don't match their words or when they seem fidgety. You can ask them questions that make them admit the truth. The key to lie detection is watching for specific tells that a person exhibits.

Many people have universal tells, such as using incongruent tenses where they switch from past to present as an indication that they are now making something up. They may change their position, the timing of their responses, or their level of eye contact.

Fidgeting and straightening out items, cleaning, or straightening their clothes are other common tells. Even the direction someone points their eyes can be a tell [15]. Learning tells is individual to each person but it is useful to know.

Chapter 6: Assertiveness

Assertiveness is one of the top most important skills in Western conversation. Assertiveness is a personality trait that comes across in communication. It is the ability to draw boundaries, make your point, defend yourself, and stand by your ideas without being aggressive or passive. You can stand up for yourself and your ideas without letting other people push you around. Assertive communication leads to better outcomes for yourself, as it makes others respect you more.

Many people will speak up when something is wrong – but they will go about it in a confrontational, aggressive way that does not win them any friends [24]. With the skills of winning people over to your way of thinking in mind, you already know that aggression is not the way to go about changing people's minds. Other people do the opposite and passively allow others to trample all over them and don't speak up when they see something wrong [24].

These people are often taken advantage of and then forgotten. They have no voice. Some people are even passive-aggressive, using sarcasm, pouting, and manipulation to get their way. These people alienate others by never speaking up about their true feelings [24]. Assertiveness lets you find a balance between these two and effectively speak up without making enemies.

When you are assertive, you respect the rights and ideas of others. But you also value your own rights, personal beliefs, thoughts, and boundaries. You won't let anyone tread on you. You possess and indicate respect for yourself and others.

Indications Of Assertiveness

You will exhibit certain traits as an assertive person. These traits are what differentiates you from aggressive, passive, and passive-aggressive people.

The first is that you are open to others' ideas. You do not tell people that they are wrong or argue yourself blue in the face. You are able to accept that others are different from you and hold different ideas. Some of these things are not worth arguing about.

You always listen to others, even if you disagree. You also respond appropriately. The ability to listen reflectively is an indicator of this. You try to reflectively listen to everybody, no matter how wrong you think they may be.

You express sincere appreciation of others. This means that you can honestly find the benefit that each person gives to the situation and thank them for that. At work, this means that you acknowledge everyone's role in the team; in social situations, you can recognize what someone brings to the conversation or what they are doing in life in general. When someone does something for you, you are grateful. The truth of life is that your success is not possible without the help of others, so you don't take that for granted. You acknowledge when someone has helped you and give credit where it is due, making others feel appreciated and valued.

You can also admit to your mistakes and apologize emphatically. You don't let pride get in the way of good social relationships. Your main goal is to recognize and correct wrongs that you may have committed. Should you do something rude or incorrect, you take ownership for your mistake and strive to make it right.

You do not consider yourself superior to others. Instead, you see yourself as an equal and you behave as such. You strive to collaborate and to work with others, as opposed to directing them and considering yourself the best in the room. This relates to appreciating others and willing to be wrong.

In all situations, you attempt to maintain confidence

and self-control. This means that you don't start crying when something upsets you, but you try to find a solution instead. You don't take your emotions out on others, you own them as your own and work on ways to solve issues that arise.

Finally, you are a master of delegation, which makes you a strong leader. You take responsibility for some things, but you know that the burden of every task cannot fall on you. You know how to assign responsibilities to others. Most people like being directed, so your ability to delegate tasks and responsibility is highly valued. Especially in work or in relationships, your willingness to provide direction can be extremely useful. Imagine a fire breaks out in a house and everyone is panicking. You don't panic, however, and you begin to tell people where to go. Your direction can save lives and help people who have lost their reasoning to panic.

Assertive Communication

When you are an assertive communicator, you tend to take more control than a passive person but you do it in a polite way, unlike aggressive communicators. You don't lose your temper and get in someone's face over something, putting the other person on the defensive and ruining any chance of collaboration. Raising your voice causes the other person to do the same, which leads to a spiral of anger that ends the communication. Assertiveness means being firm without yelling, threatening, or calling others names.

An example may be when you are accused of something you did not do at work. A passive person accepts the blame and becomes resentful, which culminates in poor work performance. An aggressive person will throw papers across the room and scream about not being responsible. An assertive person simply says, "I did not do that," and then works on finding a solution to the problem. The key difference here is that the assertive person refuses to disrespect himself by taking the blame for something he didn't do, while also handling the matter calmly and rationally.

The first step to assertive communication is owning your true feelings. If something makes you hurt or angry, don't just accept those feelings and ignore them or repress them. Don't act out in rage or hurt, either. Take a moment to acknowledge the emotion you feel and then decide how you can go about handling it by inviting collaboration with others.

Always confront people when they do wrong. This does not mean that you have to fight with people. Confrontation can be handled in a healthy way that does not entail any fighting. You first must praise the person to soften his defensiveness, then say, "I feel [insert emotion] about this. What can we do about it?"

Using "I" statements is important in assertive communication. You can see the difference between these two statements, which make the same point in different ways:

"You screwed up my files! You just cost me hours of work!"

"I am really upset right now because of a mistake with my files. Can you please help me correct it? I can show you the right way to file from now on to save us both lots of work in the future."

You use "I" statements to avoid accosting someone aggressively, hurling accusations that put them on the defensive. You don't make personal insults, such as "You always get things wrong" or "You are a mess!" Instead, you state how you feel and how you want to work on a solution. Then you invite collaboration and show the benefit you can both gain. You give the other person a buy-in to fix your problem with you.

"We" statements are also fundamental. "We" implies that you are in this together and you are working toward the same thing. It creates a sense of harmony and unity. "We can work on the filing together." This sounds better than, "You need to fix this now!"

Set clear boundaries with people. This is something people struggle with the most because they don't want to be rude or cold. Say you have a sister who is always borrowing money. It is OK to eventually tell her, "I can't lend you any more money until you pay me back." Or say you have a client who calls you in the middle of Thanksgiving dinner, berating you for not answering him sooner. You can tell him, "It is Thanksgiving and I'm enjoying dinner with my family. This matter will have to wait until tomorrow. Enjoy your holiday!" Maybe you have an uncle who feels comfortable insulting you every holiday, so you tell him, "You know, I really don't appreciate when you say that to me."

The only way people will respect your boundaries is if you enforce them. Otherwise, people will test your boundaries endlessly, hoping to break them down. Set clear rules and state them, then consistently stand by them.

When you think something, you don't remain quiet about your idea. You share it. But you do so in a way that others can appreciate. Using the skills from winning others over to your way of thinking, you make others see the wisdom of your ideas and come around to your way of thinking. This hardly means that you should have diarrhea of the mouth and blurt out whatever comes to mind. Instead, you must think about how to iterate your ideas in a way that others can understand and appreciate.

If you see something unethical happening, you are the first whistleblower. You don't just stand back and let injustice happen. "This is wrong," is all you have to say. You may be going against the stream, but your words can have an impact. Find ways to make the wrong right and you will win the respect of others.

Many people switch between passive, aggressive, and assertive. You may find it easy to be assertive with co-workers you like, but you become passive out of deference to your boss and aggressive around people you don't like. Being mindful of your responses and taking some time to think can help you remain assertive in all situations. Don't just say the first thing that comes to mind or roll over and accept poor treatment. Take a moment to think, "How can I handle this assertively?" Over time, assertiveness will become a habit that requires less thought.

Try to be as consistent as possible. If you are assertive with every person in every situation, you become an assertive person. You give others the impression that this is who you are and they can't jerk you around. People can come to rely on your assertiveness. Being inconsistent makes it hard for others to communicate with you because they don't know how you will react. People will try to take advantage of you in case you react passively and they may fear you if you sometimes act aggressively.

Delegation Skills

An assertive person possesses excellent delegation skills. Delegation skills involve assigning responsibility to the right person so that a task or mission can be completed properly. You evaluate everyone based on their personalities and skills to find who is best for what job. You accept people for who they are and use their strengths to help them actualize themselves. The ultimate benefit goes to you, because you are being a strong leader and affecting change in your life the right way.

An assertive boss will do this, finding the right people for the right jobs on a team. He knows that there is no point giving the customer service role to the person with the poorest social skills, so he finds a better role behind the scenes for that person. He uses the individual strengths of each person to get the results he needs. You must be like this in all areas of life.

An example involves setting up a household with your significant other. You may have different ideas about who must do what. You can be assertive about your beliefs and work on a compromise until you figure out who is best at keeping track of finances, doing different chores, and taking charge of the shopping. By delegating tasks to each partner, you split the workload of managing a household together.

First, determine how much ownership you want of something before you take control. Total control of something means that you take full responsibility for it. You only have total control over your own behavior; when it comes to other people, there are too many factors at play beyond your control for you to ever have total control, no matter how much you kid yourself. Before you delegate responsibilities, determine if this is even your problem and how much ownership you want. Only then can you start taking control and delegating responsibility.

Figure out who owns the problem. If you are upset because someone is marrying a person you don't like, for example, that is really your problem. The other person cannot really fix it for you. You just have to learn how to cope with the spouse you don't like and get over it. No one can be expected to reorder their lives and change their choices to help you feel better. No one is directly responsible for your happiness except you.

If someone keeps making the same mistake and does not attempt to correct it, that is their problem and you can do nothing about it. They have to fix their own problems. A problem is not yours to worry about if it does not involve you. The decisions someone makes is not up to you; therefore, it is not your problem. Another person's relationship breakdown is not your problem, for example. Stop taking ownership for problems that are not yours. When you do this, you stop overextending yourself and making people mad by meddling in their affairs.

Your emotions are always your problem. Many people say things like, "You made me feel this way, so you must fix it." The real issue is that you are not taking ownership for your own emotions when you delegate the responsibility of tending to them to others. Other people will always let you down when you expect them to fix your emotions. You must learn to handle your own emotions by confronting the person who hurt you assertively, not aggressively, and choosing a method to cope with your feelings.

When it comes to problems that you do own, you must first look into all of the facts. Never operate on assumptions. Once you have the facts, you can look into options for resolutions. Have other people present options and then evaluate them on effectiveness. This can be a group endeavor, where you ask others for opinions about which course of action is best. However, make it clear that you will decide which course of action to take in the end.

Once you have chosen a course of action, you must figure out which steps need to be taken. Then decide who can help you with each step. Tell people to delay action until you have determined the actions that will be beneficial. Also, ask people what their planned actions are so that you can evaluate how these actions fit into the overall picture and give approval. Letting people brainstorm how they will act lets everyone work together and feel like a part of the solution, creating unity and solidarity. Plus, it takes the full burden of ownership and control off of your shoulders.

Finally, give people a clear set of instructions. Give them clear approval of their intended actions. Provide a timeline for when they need to meet certain, specific goals. Expect them to fulfill these actions and then confront them if they do not. Try to find a way to make it possible for them to fulfill the actions. If someone does not deliver on a promise, for instance, don't just lose your temper. Find out why the person didn't deliver and help them find a way to deliver more successfully.

Most people find a lack of direction and control the most distracting thing in life. They can become depressed and unmotivated with no control. Taking control and giving specific instructions can motivate people again.

Let's sum all that up in an example. Your spouse comes to you saying that he is unhappy. You obviously are hurt, but you maintain self-control and ask, "Why are you unhappy?" As you find out why, you can determine if you even own this problem. You may not own it, but as the other party in the relationship, you can still take some ownership to keep your partner happy, which will obviously benefit you. Ask your partner what he wants to do to feel happier and listen carefully to the options he provides. He might say, "I want you to take more time off and spend more time with me." Then you can invite collaboration by asking him, "How do you want us to go about doing that?"

This is when you can determine how you can both go about achieving more time to spend together. You might talk to your boss about getting more personal days or coming home earlier once a week, and he can prepare to spend more time with you by working his schedule around yours. Be sure to let him know when you are simply too busy and can't be expected to make a time commitment to him. He must respect this because your work schedule is important, too.

Finally, delegate these tasks to both of you and set a timeline during which you can arrange your schedules to spend time together. Plan on some things to do together and brainstorm ideas on how to become closer. Both of you now own this problem and must fulfill your commitment to each other to spend more time together for your partner to feel happier.

Another example may be getting your child to clean his room. He will naturally be resistant to the idea. But you make your delegation clear by taking half ownership for the problem. "The house is messy and I need your help," is the way you delegate some of the responsibility to him. Then you tell him, "Go look at your room and determine what you need to clean. Then come tell me. I expect you to have those areas clean by the end of the day."

He then decides to clean up the toys scattered across his floor, so you hold him to that commitment. Tell him to put those toys in their appropriate places by the end of the day.

By the end of the day, he still has not done this. You ask him, "Why haven't you done what I asked you to do?" He says that he can't remember where toys go. This is when you take some ownership and show him where toys go, thus making it possible for him to fulfill his commitment to you.

Conclusion

If your conversations have been lackluster, then you now know how to fix that. You have learned from the very best – Dr. Robert Cialdini, Richard Bandler, and Dale Carnegie. You have the skills to make people respect and even like you through conversation.

Conversations are the essence of sharing to create a bond. You must take care not to inadvertently set up blockages in communication, or you kill conversations and relationships with one stone. You must work to keep conversations fluid and strong, so that people walk away with a good impression of you.

Since conversation is the gateway to a relationship, it is very important to let people get to know you and try to get to know other people. You can't be too negative or guarded, or you will repel potential friends. Positivity and sharing appropriate things are key. You must also find ways to keep conversations going past the ice breaker. Small talk is never as stimulating as working to find things in common or searching for relevant topics. Share stories in a good way, smile a lot, and don't condemn or criticize. Don't make the key mistakes intellectuals make and don't engage in certain habits that make you weird.

You may also use conversations to get others to come around to your way of thinking and settle differences. Never tell people that they are wrong and always treat them with respect. You will walk away from more conversations with friends instead of enemies.

Listening is a crucial component of any conversation. You should listen more than you talk. You should also engage in reflective listening to make sure you got the point. Listen with more than your ears – listen to body language and facial expressions to ascertain what a person is really communicating. Finally, you must stop thinking of what you are going to say in order to actually absorb what the other person is trying to say.

To truly improve your conversations, you must be assertive. Assertiveness is key to being a good person and making others respect you. You must respect yourself and others and stand up for what is right. You must set boundaries and delegate tasks based on what the other person is capable of doing. Don't own problems that are not yours.

Practice makes perfect. Putting these new skills to use can help you elevate your conversations from blah to awesome. As you start to make friends and partners with great conversation, you will see the benefits of your hard work. Good conversation will make your life so much better. Don't put off polishing your conversation skills, or you will continue to miss out on some great opportunities to know great people.

References

1 Apperle, Robin, et al. *Neural responses to maternal praise and criticism: Relationship to depression and anxiety symptoms in high-risk adolescent girls.* Neuroimage Clin. 2016; 11: 548–554. Published online 2016 Apr 4. doi: 10.1016/j.nicl.2016.03.009.

2 Bradbury, Travis. *How Complaining Rewires Your Brain for Negativity.* TalentSmart. https://www.huffpost.com/entry/how-complaining-rewires-y_n_13634470.

3 Kini, P., et al. *The Effects of Gratitude Expression on Neural Activity.* Neorimage. 2016 Mar;128:1-10. doi: 10.1016/j.neuroimage.2015.12.040. Epub 2015 Dec 30.

4 Cialdini, R. (2008). *Influence: The Psychology of Persuasion, 5th Ed.* Allyn and Bacon. ISBN-13: 9 78-0061241895

5 Carnegie, Dale. *How to Win Friends and Influence People*. Pocket Books. 1998. ISBN-13: 978-0671027032.

6 Carmody, Dennis & Lewis, Michael. *Brain Activation When Hearing One's Own And Others' Names*. Brain Res. 2006 Oct 20; 1116(1): 153–158.

7 Carolyn Parkinson, Adam M. Kleinbaum, & Thalia Wheatley. *Similar Neural Responses Predict Friendship*. Journal Of Nature Communications, Vol 9, Article # 332. 2018.

8 Maslow, A. H. (1943). A theory of human motivation. *Psychological Review, 50*(4), 370-396. http://dx.doi.org/10.1037/h0054346

9 Stamp, Glen, Vangelesti, Anita, & Daly, John. *The Creation of Defensiveness in Social Interaction.*

Communication Quarterly, Vol. 40, No. 2, Spring 1992, Pages 1 77-19.

10 O'Doherty, J., et al. *Beauty of a Smile: The Role of the Medial Orbitofrontal Cortex in Facial Attractiveness.* Neuropsychologica. 2003. Vol. 41, pp. 147-155. https://pure.mpg.de/rest/items /item_2614428/component/file_2623264/content

11 Roberts, Steven, et al. *Making Boundaries Great Again: Essentialism and Support for Boundary-Enhancing Initiatives.* Personality and Social Psychology Bulletin. 2017. https://doi.org/10.1177/0146167217724801

12 Foti, Dan, et al. *Differentiating Neural Responses to Emotional Pictures: Evidence from Temporal-Spatial PCA.* Psychopsychology. 2009. Vol 49, pp. 521-530. DOI: 0.1111/j.1469-8986.2009.00796.x.

13 Mayben, Simon. *Busting The Attention Span Myth.* BBC News. March 10, 2017. Https://Www.Bbc.Com/News/Health-38896790.

14 Tosun, S., Et Al. *Is An Ideal Sense Of Humor Gendered? A Cross-National Study.* Front Psychol. 2018; 9: 199.

Published online 2018 Feb 27. doi: 10.3389/fpsyg.2018.00199

15 Bandler, R., Roberti, A., & Fitzpatrick, O. (2013). *The Ultimate Introduction To NLP: How To Build A Successful Life.* Harpercollins. ISBN: 978-0007497416.

16 Fowler, James H. And Nicholas A. Christakis. 2008. *Dynamic Spread Of Happiness In A Large Social Network: Longitudinal Analysis Over 20 Years In The Framingham Heart Study.* British

Medical Journal 337,No. A2338: 1-9

17 Saxton, T., Caryl, P., & Roberts, S. (2006). *Vocal and facial attractiveness judgments of children, adolescents and adults: The ontogeny of mate choice.* Ethology, 112(12), 1179–1185. doi:10.1111/j.1439-0310.2006.01278.x

18 Gallup, G. R., & Frederick, D. A. (2010). *The science of sex appeal: An evolutionary perspective.* Review of General Psychology, 14(3), 240–250. doi:10.1037/a0020451

19 Fraccaro, P. J., Jones, B. C., Vukovic, J., Smith, F. G., Watkins, C. D., Feinberg, D. R., & ... DeBruine, L. M. (2011). *Experimental evidence that women speak in a higher voice pitch to men they find attractive.* Journal of Evolutionary Psychology, 9(1), 57–67. doi:10.1556/JEP.9.2011.33.1

20 Ophir, Eyal, et al. *Cognitive Control in Media Multitaskers.* 2009. Stanford Research. https://www.pnas.org/content/pnas/106/37/15583.full.pdf.

21 *Types of Listening.* Changing Minds. http://changingminds.org/techniques/listening/types_listening.htm.

22 Harry Weger Jr., Gina Castle Bell, Elizabeth M. Minei & Melissa C. Robinson (2014) The Relative Effectiveness of Active Listening in Initial Interactions, International Journal of Listening, 28:1, 13-31, DOI: 10.1080/10904018.2013.813234

23 Yaffe, Philip. *The 7% Rule: Fact, Fiction, or Misunderstanding.* Ubiquity. Volume 2011, Number October (2011), Pages 1-5. DOI: 10.1145/2043155.2043156.

24 Mayo Clinic Staff. *Being Assertive: Reduce Stress, Communicate Better.* 2019. https://www.mayoclinic.org/healthy-lifestyle/stress-management/in-depth/assertive/art-20044644.

Disclaimer

The information contained in this book and its components, is meant to serve as a comprehensive collection of strategies that the author of this book has done research about. Summaries, strategies, tips and tricks are only recommendations by the author, and reading this book will not guarantee that one's results will exactly mirror the author's results.

The author of this book has made all reasonable efforts to provide current and accurate information for the readers of this book. The author and its associates will not be held liable for any unintentional errors or omissions that may be found.

The material in the book may include information by third parties. Third party materials comprise of opinions expressed by their owners. As such, the author of this book does not assume responsibility or liability for any third party material or opinions.

The publication of third party material does not constitute the author's guarantee of any information, products, services, or opinions contained within third party material. Use of third party material does not guarantee that your results will mirror our results. Publication of such third party material is simply a recommendation and expression of the author's own opinion of that material.

Whether because of the progression of the Internet, or the unforeseen changes in company policy and editorial submission guidelines, what is stated as fact at the time of this writing may become outdated or inapplicable later.

written expressed and signed permission from the author.

Made in the USA
Middletown, DE
05 July 2020